Body
Happy
Kids

MOLLY FORBES

Body Happy Kids

HOW TO HELP CHILDREN AND TEENS LOVE THE SKIN THEY'RE IN

Vermilion
LONDON

Vermilion, an imprint of Ebury Publishing,
20 Vauxhall Bridge Road,
London SW1V 2SA

Vermilion is part of the Penguin Random House group of companies
whose addresses can be found at global.penguinrandomhouse.com

Penguin
Random House
UK

Copyright © Molly Forbes 2021
Illustrations © Stacie Swift 2021

Molly Forbes has asserted her right to be identified as the author of this
Work in accordance with the Copyright, Designs and Patents Act 1988

First published by Vermilion in 2021

www.penguin.co.uk

A CIP catalogue record for this book is available from the British Library

ISBN 9781785043581

Typeset in 10.75/15.6 pt Bembo Std
by Integra Software Services Pvt. Ltd, Pondicherry

Printed and bound in Great Britain by Clays Ltd, Elcograf S.p.A.

The authorised representative in the EEA is Penguin Random House Ireland,
Morrison Chambers, 32 Nassau Street, Dublin D02 YH68.

Penguin Random House is committed to a sustainable future for our business, our readers and our planet. This book is made from Forest Stewardship Council® certified paper.

For Freya, Effie, Erin, George, Ella and Felix.
May you always know how lovely you are.

Contents

We're Not Born Hating Our Bodies

We are not born hating our bodies. I don't think I appreciated this statement fully until I became a mother and saw for myself how distinctly unbothered babies are by what the world thinks of them (#BeMoreBaby should be a thing). Both my daughters came out of my body with an unquestioning instinct for what made their own bodies feel good. Loudly, often in the middle of the night, they would tell me when they were hungry and, once they'd filled their bellies, they'd drift off into a milky state of bliss. Then they'd wake up, play, shout for more milk and sleep again. I'd look at their tiny fingernails, the soft pulsating point on the top of their skulls, their little feet kicking wildly at the world, and would feel an icy slither of anger at the thought that anyone or anything would ever make them feel even a hint less than absolutely perfect.

My snoozing, milk-drunk babies lived happily in the experience of their bodies every day. They didn't look down at

1

their stomachs or peer round at their bums and think of these body parts as somehow separate to themselves, needing to be trained or moulded or trimmed down. And, as toddlers, they raced unselfconsciously towards the pool and jumped into the water with absolute unquestioning freedom. They were yet to see their bodies as works in progress or something to improve. They appreciated their bodies for what they could do. They didn't gaze wistfully at the models in fashion magazines or the footballers on telly and wish they looked like them. They didn't even notice them to begin with.

When you stop to think about all the messages telling us that our bodies aren't good enough just as they are, it's a miracle anyone feels good in the skin they're in – and an even bigger miracle that babies seem to get out of it all relatively unscathed. But what if, without even realising it, we're contributing to the feelings of body doubt and the culture of comparison our sons and daughters are experiencing when they're as young as three years old? The messages telling us that our bodies are a problem are everywhere, and our children are not immune to them. The messages aren't just on TV, in magazines or on social media; they're in the home, at school and in the playground too.

The good news is that, once you know the problem, it's easier to find the solution – half the battle is spotting the issue in the first place. I'm going to help you with this by shining a light on the negative messages (because they're not always easy to identify), sharing ideas on how to counteract them and offering clear, evidence-based, inspiring tools to boost your kids' body happiness and make them feel fabulous just as they are. I have no doubt some of what you read will also help you to feel better in your own skin too.

HOW I CAME TO WRITE THIS BOOK

If you're reading this thinking that it's all going to be an uphill battle, please don't despair. I wrote this book from the perspective of someone who was most definitely (and unwittingly) part of the problem, standing in the way between my children and their own body confidence. A few years ago, I had to explain to my five-year-old daughter why I was weighing spinach. It wasn't any old spinach – it was organic, baby leaf spinach, as specified by the latest 'healthy eating' fad I was embarking on in order to have a flatter stomach for our first family holiday abroad later that year. In my quest for a smaller, tighter, smoother body I didn't notice my daughter watching me stepping on the scales each morning or sucking my tummy in critically when I looked in the mirror. I was so consumed by the idea that I needed to 'get healthy', I didn't realise that what I was doing wasn't actually very healthy at all.

'Mummy, why are you weighing spinach?' was my lightbulb moment. In that second I realised I didn't have a rational answer for my daughter; 'Because I want to be slimmer so I can wear a bikini on holiday, because you should only really enjoy the feeling of the sun on your belly if your belly is small and firm,' didn't seem like a sensible response. And so began my first tentative steps towards body acceptance.

As soon as I started to feel good about my body – wobbles and all – I also started to notice all the things trying to drag me back down. And, in the process, I began to be aware of all the messages trying to drag my children down too. From the Disney princesses who all have one type of body to the diet chat from parents in the playground on the way into school. From the lack of representation in picture books to the stories

3

and TV shows equating 'fat' with 'lazy'. From the simplified lessons on nutrition telling children that some food is 'good' and some food is 'bad' to the filters their friends are applying on their own social media photos. These messages are everywhere.

I'm not an academic or a clinician, but I am a journalist and a mum who just wants to know the best way to help my daughters avoid ever feeling the need to weigh spinach as I did. I want my children – and yours – to always feel like they're enough, just as they are. So I set out on a journey to try to find the best way to raise body happy kids and unpick some of the messages I'd spent a lifetime learning. And I did it the only way I know how: by talking to people.

My travels took me on to *Naked Beach* – a prime-time, pre-watershed body-confidence-boosting TV show based on a social experiment devised by Dr Keon West from Goldsmiths University – where I was one of the hosts helping a group of guests overcome their own body insecurities. In 2019 I appeared on telly in nothing but body paint. There was a moment, when we were doing promo for the show, when I got lost in the corridors of Television Centre wearing nothing but a thong and body paint, trying to find my way back to the green room before we went on the *This Morning* sofa!

My search for answers continued in a new podcast all about body image called *Body Cons*, which I co-hosted alongside my friend, writer and trainee counsellor Lottie Storey, and where we interviewed academics and activists, campaigners and doctors, models and mental health advocates. I started campaigning on the issue too, founding the #FreeFromDiets campaign, calling for tighter restrictions in the way diet brands and weight-loss products advertise around children, and running workshops for teachers and youth workers.

But the deeper I delved into the subject, the more confusing it all became. I noticed diet brands disguising themselves as health products, beauty brands co-opting the body-positivity movement to sell anti-cellulite cream, and detox teas using the wellness trend to shift teabags containing laxatives. And the more parents I spoke to, the more I realised all these messages around health and beauty were confusing for us all; on the one hand we want our kids to grow up confident, but on the other we think maybe we should put our child on a diet because they were weighed at school and we had a letter home saying their BMI is too high.

We regularly hear about rising levels of 'childhood obesity' and the dangers of 'junk' food. But did you also know that in the last decade the number of pre-teens being treated for anorexia has doubled, that one in five girls isn't raising her hand in class for fear of being judged for how she looks, and that one in eight adults has felt suicidal because they are so unhappy with their appearance?[1] Low body confidence is a public health problem just as serious as other health issues, yet it regularly gets left out of the media headlines.

We're often presented with one idea of health, but it's about more than just what you eat and how much you move your body. While conversations around mental health are becoming less taboo, there's still a huge lack of public awareness about how body image is linked to mental health and the impact these feelings can have on the way we interact with our friends and perform at school and in work.[2] And while researchers tell us that evidence shows the better we feel about our bodies (regardless of what they look like), the more likely we are to do things that feel good for our body[3], this is often a point ignored by the mainstream media selling the narrative that health only looks one way.

Making children feel good about their bodies, right now, as it is, will have a direct impact on how they treat their bodies. Experts also warn that body shaming – and telling kids that their bodies are 'wrong' – makes children feel bad about their bodies, which in turn can lead to them not wanting to join in sport at school or take part in team exercise. In the process of trying to encourage our children to 'be healthy', there's a high chance our efforts might be having the opposite effect. I know – my mind was blown by all this too.

WHO IS THIS BOOK FOR?

This book is for any adult who is ever around children. You might be a parent, grandparent, guardian, carer, teacher, child-minder, Brownies or Scouts leader, or dance teacher. You might have younger brothers or sisters or be an aunt or uncle. Even if you're not regularly around children, if you want to be involved in changing the culture the next generation of kids are growing up in, then this book is for you too. Everyone is welcome here.

I write this book from my perspective as a heterosexual, straight-sized, nondisabled white woman who identifies as the gender I was assigned at birth and grew up in the eighties and nineties. Throughout the book I share many of my own experiences of body image and diet culture, which may not be the same as yours. Living in the body that I do means that while (like all of us) I've been a victim of diet culture, the way it's impacted me is not the same as the way it's impacted many others. I've never been to the doctor with a sore throat, for example, and been told to lose weight. I can buy clothes in my size in pretty much every high-street clothes shop I go into. And, as far as I'm aware, I've not been turned down for job interviews because of the size, shape, colour or ability of my body. And my children are growing up with the same privileges.

However, body image impacts all of us – if you have a body, then you have a body image. And I care deeply about changing the culture that allows any child to question their body. I don't have all the answers, which is why I've included many different voices throughout this book to help explore the issue of body image and how we can raise children who feel better in their skin. From activists to academics, health professionals to educators, I hope the range of people who've contributed to this book may go some way to helping us all understand how we can help our kids grow up liking their bodies, whatever their bodies look like and whatever their bodies can do.

If you've struggled with your own body image issues in the past, or are recovering from a troubled relationship with eating or exercise, then please be aware that I discuss some of my own experiences in this book that may be difficult for you to read. At the end of this book you'll find a list of resources, charities and counselling services which will be helpful in case you are in need of extra support overcoming these issues (see page 233).

HOW TO USE THIS BOOK

At the end of each chapter you'll find a body image boosting exercise you can do at home with your children (and by yourself). Some of these things can be incorporated into your daily routine and some will be specific activities you can tailor depending on the age of your child. You'll also find lots of resources as you read through the book which will inspire you to keep building a body happy environment around your children, helping to boost their resilience to the messages they will undoubtedly be bombarded with as they move through life.

My hope is that you'll read this book now, then refer back to it lots over the years to come, using the tools and reminding yourself of ways you can help your kids as they grow and as the challenges they face around their bodies inevitably change. I've written the book with those who are short on time (basically everyone I know!) in mind so you can easily skip to a relevant section based on what your child is going through right now, or read it all in one go, or just dip in and out of it as and when you need to.

A note about language

The word 'fat' is, in essence, just a neutral, descriptive word, exactly the same as 'thin' or 'tall' or 'short'. But because body ideals and fatphobia are deeply embedded in our culture, this is still a word that often comes loaded with negative connotations. We're going to explore this in more depth in Chapter 4, where we'll also hear from people reclaiming the word 'fat' and challenging the ideas and stigma surrounding it. We're going to delve further into how the language that adults use to describe bodies and the way our bodies function can impact the way children feel about their own bodies, and look at some of the messages perpetuating 'fat' as bad.

We also can't talk about body image and kids without mentioning 'obesity' because the narrative around health and weight is one of the biggest obstacles to children feeling at peace in their bodies. However, many people find this word problematic, arguing that it perpetuates weight stigma because it gives a medical name to being in a bigger body and labels it as a problem, creating a sense of otherness and reinforcing a hierarchy of body types. For this reason, when I use this word it will always be in quotation marks, as it will often be quoted directly from another source.

WELCOME TO *BODY HAPPY KIDS*

Body Happy Kids isn't just about raising children who don't compare themselves unfavourably to the images in magazines. And it's not just about creating a future generation of adults who have sky-high levels of self-confidence. It's about giving our children the chance, right now, to continue to move their bodies for joy in just the way they did as a baby. It's about giving our children the chance to thrive at school and take part in activities that bring them happiness, even if they don't look like the celebrities they admire or have bodies that fit the picture of health we're often presented with. It's about raising children who don't make judgements about others based on the way they look.

We're not born hating our bodies and, hopefully with this book, our children will never need to relearn how to be friends with their bodies in the first place.

CHAPTER 1

What Does Positive Body Image Look Like?*

What exactly is body image? How is it measured? Why does it matter? And when does it all begin? You'll find the answers to all these questions and more in this chapter. We're going to hear from people whose job it is to research the subject of body image, as well as some pretty sobering stats which show that how children feel about their bodies can impact their lives in many ways.

Some of what you're about to read might surprise you, some of it might make you feel sad and some might make you feel angry. But there will also be an overriding sense of hope, as you learn some practical tools to empower the kids in your life to feel good (with the added bonus that it might make you feel better too!).

---

* Spoiler: It's not just liking what you see in the mirror.

The moment of realisation

Do you remember the first time you questioned your body? Look back into your past and, somewhere, there will have been a moment. It might have been a comment from a relative or a kid in the playground. It could have been the dawning realisation that none of your favourite book or TV characters looked like you, or it might have been a whisper from a doctor or the school nurse that made you look down at your body and view it as a problem, rather than just a part of yourself.

My moment came somewhere around the age of 12. I'd navigated the potential body image issues of childhood relatively unscathed. Despite being raised in the eighties and nineties, when the diet industry was booming and the lack of representation in the mainstream media was even narrower than today, I was probably fairly unusual in having parents who never body shamed themselves or others, emphasised what I could do over how I looked, and were pretty vigilant about the types of toys I played with and the sorts of shows I watched on telly.

But I didn't grow up in a cave on top of a hill wearing ear plugs and a blindfold so, somewhere along the way, the constant messages around me seeped in. I heard other adults talking about diets; I read 'simple weight-loss tips' in magazines; I noticed how the people held up by society as successful and beautiful and healthy all looked one way, and I didn't have the resilience or tools at hand to decode some of these messages and let them bounce off me.

As a skinny kid with 'swimmer's shoulders' I worried my boobs weren't big enough to make boys fancy me, then later, aged 15, I revelled in the fact that I could fit into a size 6 bikini on holiday and soaked up the compliments from other teenagers about my flat tummy. I was quite hungry that summer. It never blossomed into a full-blown issue, but I bounced on and off the diet wagon in a gentle sort of way throughout my late teens and early twenties. And I never felt fully free of this annoying buzz of doubt around my body or stopped to challenge it completely, until I became a mother.

Spinach-gate, as I now think of it, was my turning point, and it's when I first became aware of 'body image' as a thing that can affect many different areas of life. Growing up as a teenager I wasn't aware of ideas around 'body confidence', 'body acceptance' or 'body positivity'. I just thought it was a given that if you had a body, you'd want to change it some-how. This idea lasted right through to my thirties and that light-bulb moment when I realised I had a choice: I could either continue to seek happiness, confidence and health by changing the shape of my body, or I could work on changing my mindset instead.

Gradually, I started to swap the body work for mind work. I began to make little tweaks to my life by changing who I was following online, and investing my time in podcasts and books that challenged the belief that my body was the most important thing about me, and that in order to be happy, successful and healthy I needed to look a certain way. You can't unlearn a lifetime of negative messages overnight – and it was definitely 'work' in that it didn't come easy – but I began to notice a return on my investment: I was starting to feel better.

I discovered that once I gave up trying to tone, shrink and mould my body into another shape, I could live a fuller, happier, healthier life – just like the days when I was a gurgling baby with a saggy nappy and no care for how many rolls were on my belly (#BeMoreBaby). I started to wear different clothes,

13

stopped obsessing about 'good' and 'bad' food, discovered a new love of exercise (movement is actually really fun when you do it for how it makes you feel over how it makes you look) and began to feel properly alive, confident and at home in my body again.

WHAT IS BODY IMAGE?

Experts define body image as a person's emotional attitudes, beliefs and perceptions of their own body. Put simply, body image is about how you think and feel about the way your body looks, and in turn how you treat your body. It's about how you value yourself and your ability to separate that value from how you look. When I appeared on TV in body paint as one of the hosts of *Naked Beach* I felt completely happy and comfortable in my body, not because I thought I looked the bomb, but because I knew, finally, that the way I looked and the shape of my body were not what mattered. Ironically, my positive body image had very little to do with what my body looked like at all.

In fact, in their book *Beauty Around the World: A Cultural Encyclopedia*, Erin Kenny and Elizabeth Gackstetter Nichols discuss how the arrival of the modern bathroom in western cultures in the late nineteenth century meant, 'Cleanliness was medicalised as hygiene which also translated to the maintenance of an attractive appearance to others.'[1] The more mirrors became readily available, the more we could look in them and find fault with what we saw. And now, in the age of the smartphone, the selfie and the filter, the focus is on how we look more than ever, creating a heightened obsession with appearance that didn't exist before. Some academics say there's a chance this could be bad news for body image because the more we look at ourselves, the worse we end up feeling about our bodies.[2] This is because we are objectifying ourselves through a hypercritical lens and comparing ourselves to an ideal.

Within the walls of some universities, there are teams of researchers dedicated to studying the subject of body image. This is not a new subject, but the constantly changing social and environmental landscape does mean the goalposts are always shifting. Academics studying body image 20 years ago wouldn't have had to factor in the effects of social media, for example.

One thing that doesn't change though is what a positive body image looks like – or doesn't look like. Because, despite what the adverts co-opting the body acceptance movement tell us, changing the appearance of your body won't necessarily change how you feel about it.

'Positive body image is more than liking how you look,' explains Nadia Craddock, PhD, a body image researcher at the Centre for Appearance Research at the University of the West of England. 'It's about appreciating your body for what it allows you to do, respecting and looking after your body, accepting your body regardless of how it matches up to any societal appearance ideal, and it's also about feeling at home in your body and connected with it.'

When researchers are studying body image they look at lots of different ways of thinking about our relationship with our bodies. Older studies used to use 'body satisfaction' (liking what you see in the mirror) as a measure of positive body image, while today academics tend to measure 'body appreciation' (appreciating what your body can do). Nadia explains that while body satisfaction and body appreciation are not the same thing, they do both fall under the umbrella of positive body image. Research does show though, that getting too hung up on what you see in the mirror (even if you enjoy what's looking back at you) can actually lead to poor body image, via preoccupation with appearance. This could explain the thing about the bathrooms and the mirrors and the smartphones.

'A big component of negative body image is body dissatisfaction – so not liking the way your body looks,' says Nadia. 'This is often accompanied with trying to change your body in some way. Other components of negative body image include things like an "over-evaluation" of your appearance – when we assign excessive importance on our appearance in our overall evaluations of self and excessive preoccupation with our appearance, which might involve constantly checking and scrutinising our appearance. This is linked to the idea of self-objectification, where we view ourselves from the perspective of an external viewer or through the "male gaze". According to Objectification Theory, this can lead to what is termed "self-surveillance" – the practice of continually monitoring and checking our bodies to see if they are "good enough". In turn, this can lead to body shame and feeling anxious about our appearance.'

But how does all this relate to kids? As a child I don't remember obsessing in front of the mirror, unless it was to practise pop songs or the latest dance routine I'd seen on *Top of the Pops*. And now as a mum I see this same pattern emerging with my own children (although they've replaced the Macarena with whatever dance craze has gone viral this week).

In fact, many toy manufacturers include mirrors and reflective surfaces in their toys for babies and toddlers, and parents are often encouraged to use mirrors as part of sensory play, as experts say babies love to look at their own reflections – although it's not until around the age of 18 months that they recognise it's their own face looking back at them.[3] So at what

16

point do children learn to start equating their worth as a person with what is facing them in the mirror? And should parents of older children do away with mirrors altogether? Well, like many things, it's not that straightforward.

'Body image is a psychological construct, so it's about our internal relationship with our bodies. That said, it's important to recognise that body image is informed by societal ideals promoted by media and advertising, and by systems of oppression such as racism or fatphobia,' explains Nadia.

We'll explore this idea more towards the end of the chapter, but for now it's important to know that the way we think and feel about our bodies are often informed by whatever society tells us is the 'perfect body' of the moment. In the US and UK, for example, we've had various different bodies held up as the ideal for women, from Marilyn Monroe's hourglass curves in the fifties, Twiggy's thin frame of the sixties and Farrah Fawcett's athletic, svelte shape of the seventies, all the way through to the era that I grew up in – the nineties – when it was all about the 'waif look', which Kate Moss embodied. Most recently, it's back to round breasts and bums, with tiny waists, as Kim Kardashian's body has become the ideal. The 'perfect body' of the moment, then, will vary depending on where you live in the world or what era you're growing up in, because ideals change and aren't the same everywhere. But ultimately, says Nadia, if there's a 'perfect body' being promoted, then there's an assumption that we'll be striving towards achieving it in some way. And it's this process – this pursuit of striving towards something society says is good – that can lead to problems when it comes to body image.

'Sociocultural theory helps us understand how we get from societal appearance ideals to negative body image (and disordered eating). The most widely established evidence-based model currently is the Tripartite Influence model, which theorises that appearance pressures to meet or move closer to societal appearance ideals from the media, family and friends leads to body dissatisfaction through two key processes. The first is internalisation where we "buy-into" or "subscribe" to the idea that there is an ideal appearance and believe that in order to be desirable, happy, good, popular and attractive, we need to look a certain way. The second is upward appearance comparisons, comparing our bodies to those we deem more attractive in some way,' says Nadia. 'This process of comparisons leads to us feeling worse about our bodies because, when we are comparing ourselves to an unrealistic ideal (e.g. to someone younger than us, with a different body type, whose image has been digitally edited, etc.), we will inevitably find ourselves falling short in some way.'

So back to the mirrors – maybe it's not a case of getting rid of them altogether, but instead learning to look into them in a different way, through our own eyes and not the lens of society's idealised tinted spectacles. If we can start to take back the power and look at our bodies through new, kinder, more accepting eyes, this will have a huge impact on our children.

'It's helpful to think how we can disrupt the three sources of societal appearance pressures for children,' says Nadia. 'First, we can show acceptance of our children's bodies, regardless of how they reflect any societal ideal. Research has shown this is one of the most important factors when it comes to children's body image – acceptance of their bodies by their friends and family members. Family members modelling acceptance of their own bodies is also important. Second, we can also have a zero tolerance approach to appearance-based teasing at home and at school. Third, we can ensure the media our children consume shows and celebrates appearance diversity.'

And this idea of acceptance leads us back to the idea of positive body image. 'There are lots of terms that get thrown up,' explains Nadia. 'People talk about body neutrality, body acceptance, body respect, body freedom, body liberation, etc. All these terms refer to a bigger idea of feeling at home in your body, not subscribing to an ideal or chasing an ideal. It's all about gratitude, appreciation and embodiment.'

Rewind back to my spinach-weighing days and I was most definitely not at home with, connected to or appreciative of my body. I ignored my feelings of hunger, battled on through exercise that physically hurt me and spent far too much time on the scales or in front of the mirror. And while I was sucking in my tummy and checking my body from different angles? My kids were watching. I forgot that the way I talked to myself mattered, and that this could have an impact on how my children felt about their own bodies too.

WHEN DOES BODY IMAGE BEGIN?

While a baby isn't aware of the Kim Kardashian bum and doesn't feel the pressure to have 'on fleek' brows, researchers have found that children as young as three years old can have body image issues.[4] A 2015 study in the US found that 34 per cent of five-year-old girls are on a diet and almost half of the children studied wanted to be thinner.[5]

Another study in the same year from US non-profit organisation Common Sense Media found that one half of girls and one third of boys aged six to eight years had an 'ideal weight' and it was thinner than their current one.[6] This study also found that by the age of six many children were aware of dieting and some had already tried it. And in the UK, a 2016 report from the Professional Association for Childcare and Early Years found that children as young as three were displaying body confidence issues.[7] The report found that 24 per cent of childcare providers had noticed body image dilemmas from kids aged between just three and five years old, with that figure almost doubling by the time children reached the ages of six to ten years old.

Before anyone assumes these issues are confined to girls, reports from The Children's Society have shown that, although girls have traditionally struggled with body image issues more, boys are now catching up.[8] The Good Childhood Report in 2020 found 'a significant increase in the proportion of boys unhappy with their appearance' and the 2019 report stated that one in twelve boys feels miserable about the way he looks. Overall, the 2019 report found that a quarter of a million children in the UK are unhappy, with appearance listed as one of the key things they worry about.

Some psychologists suggest the gap might be even smaller, saying that it's not that boys don't worry about body image, more that they might not always have the vocabulary to express how they're feeling.[9] This isn't necessarily their fault though; there are various studies which found that the language adults use around children to express emotions can differ depending on the gender of the child.[10] So if boys aren't being given the opportunity to discuss how they're feeling, or they're told they should (or shouldn't) be feeling a certain way, it stands to reason they might hide their emotions or not have the right tools to discuss them in the first place. And with body image typically being seen as a 'girly' issue, one explanation for the gender gap could be that boys just don't want to admit feeling bad about their bodies, even if it's causing them real angst.

While we don't know the exact age children develop body image, we do know that very young children can already demonstrate anti-fat bias and compare their bodies to others, and these feelings are making them unhappy. And we also know that body image issues can affect children of all genders.

Psychologists have found that children can start to understand how they fit into social groups between the tender ages of 18 and 30 months, so before they're even three years old they can identify their gender and age, and recognise physical characteristics such as 'strong'.[11] This is known as 'self-concept development'. What's more, they can also show emotions such as pride, embarrassment or shame, suggesting that toddlers are aware of other people's social reactions to them in much the same way as adults. Developmental psychologists argue this is the beginning of social comparison, which is a big deal when it comes to body image.

In my campaigning work this is a theme that comes up again and again. I hear from so many parents and teachers reporting issues with the children in their care saying their bodies are 'not good enough' or worrying about wearing certain clothes, or being singled out at school for the way they look, or announcing they need to 'go on a diet'. I've heard from mums whose ten-year-old sons are suddenly obsessed with following YouTube workouts to get big muscles and Reception teachers seeking advice on how to handle kids in their class saying their 'tummy is too big'. And with my own kids, I know the school curriculum and messaging around 'healthy eating' can sometimes be confusing and has, in the past, led them to question their own bodies.

Being aware of body image as a subject, then, isn't something we can just put off until our children are teenagers. We can't just assume we don't need to know about this stuff until our children reach the age of 13 when they want a phone and an Instagram account and to read magazines featuring airbrushed images of their favourite celebrities. Arguably, by this age the foundations for their body insecurities have already long since been laid.

WHY DOES BODY IMAGE MATTER?

On the morning of 27 June 2010 I lay in a stuffy maternity ward on the hottest day of the year, a dazed new mum in complete awe of the perfect baby who had just come out of my body. That icy stab of anger I felt that anyone would ever make my baby feel anything less than perfect was, perhaps, entirely justified. In those early baby and toddler days I may not have been tuned into the various body image insecurities that could befall my daughters as they grew, but being the mum of girls I had already experienced plenty of occasions when my babies were called 'pretty' or 'beautiful' while their baby boy peers were called 'clever' or 'strong'.

I'd wandered through the shops and seen aisle upon aisle of pink babygrows with slogans like 'little princess' while the tiny baby boys' clothes had words like 'hero' plastered across them. And I'd been given the fairy-tale books for my babies featuring slim, wide-eyed princesses being rescued by toned, 'brave' princes. OK, so my babies weren't explicitly being told to 'take up as little space as possible and be pretty', but the expectation was placed on them as soon as they entered the world. And if my babies had been boys? The weight of perfection was equally heavy – it was their job to be fierce, strong and brave.

These early stereotypes all have an impact on kids' body image later on because they lay the early groundwork for body ideals, perpetuating the idea that girls should be quiet and pretty and boys should be loud and strong. This is bad news, both for gender conforming and gender non-conforming children. But in a society where conversations about diets are as common as conversations about the weather, and where it's completely normal to want to change your body, why does it even matter if a kid feels bad about their body? And how can we clearly spot if a child has negative body image?

We know that having a negative body image can affect a child's life in all sorts of ways. For some children it may simply be equating 'fat' with 'bad' from an early age, while for others it may be refusing certain types of food for fear of putting on weight. This early weight bias can then play a role in how children eat – and in some cases trigger serious mental health concerns such as disordered eating or eating disorders, body dysmorphic disorder, anxiety and depression. The Mental Health Foundation's 2019 body image report found that one in eight adults has suffered suicidal thoughts or feelings because of their body image, and that when children and teenagers feel bad about their bodies they're more likely to display 'risk-taking behaviours' such as going on a diet, considering cosmetic surgery or taking steroids.[12]

'The experience of children can be seen as passive fatphobia,' explains Harley Street eating disorder and body image therapist Laura Phelan. 'With passive smoking, children are exposed to the smoke if they're in the room when Mum or Dad smokes. And when parents are talking about their bodies in a negative way, they may not be saying that directly to the child, but as the child takes in that information, they start to think about it for themselves. So that's why we often hear children getting anxious around their bodies. And they're not even at the age when they're able to cognitively compartmentalise these ideas yet. They don't understand it's an issue for their mum or their dad. They're thinking it must be an issue for them too.'

These anxieties spread quickly, says Laura: 'Children are so influential. They're spreading what adults' ideas of body ideals have put on them. So once you say to one kid that it's bad to be fat, that child's telling the whole class and the fear will spread like wildfire amongst children.'

It's a complicated issue though, because the outcomes of negative body image can show up in a variety of ways. 'Many people with eating disorders such as bulimia and binge eating, for example, are doing so because of ideas around the owner-ship and safety of their bodies,' explains Laura. 'People might binge eat, for example, to keep their bodies bigger because it feels safer – they won't be so preyed on, because they've learned from a young age that to be bigger is to be less attractive. Often people who've experienced trauma may want to change how their bodies look, or abuse their bodies, as a way to protect it. This idea also applies to thinness. For many people, look-ing emaciated and smaller, taking up less space physically and literally being less seen and staying hidden, is a way to protect themselves. We need to have more narratives around sexual-ity, the ownership of bodies – particularly young girls – and get away from this idea that as you grow it's OK for people to start commenting on your body and take ownership of it. This causes all sorts of problems on an individual level for the body image and mental health of children.'

It's not just the serious mental health issues that we need to worry about though. Research also shows that low body image

can mean young children might want to cover up parts of their bodies because they feel self-conscious or they may not want to get changed at school for PE. And for others, they may attempt to avoid sport altogether. For example, in their 2017 'Girls' Attitudes Survey', Girlguiding UK found that 43 per cent of the girls they questioned don't join in sport for fear of being judged over their appearance.[13] And a 2018 study in the US found that teenagers who feel bad about their appearance are more likely to smoke and binge drink.[14] Body image issues aren't just bad for mental health – they're bad for physical health too.

In a world where we're regularly encouraging our kids to 'be their best self' or 'live their best life' we need to recognise that this is often pretty hard if the vessel taking our children from A to B every day, enabling them to live their life, is something they're being taught to question, distrust – or even hate. You can't embrace every experience and opportunity that comes your way if you're distracted by negative thoughts about your body.

Away from mental and physical health, body image issues can impact kids in other ways that seem so basic it's almost too obvious. But if you've ever felt like pulling a duvet day because of what's looking back at you in the mirror, then you'll understand. Researchers say that the way our children think and feel about their bodies is directly affecting how they engage in class – or even if they turn up for school in the first place.[15]

Dr Melissa Atkinson is a researcher and lecturer in the psychology department at the University of Bath. 'Global surveys conducted by the Dove Self-Esteem Project found that the majority of girls were opting out of a number of different activities due to not feeling good about the way they look, and some of those activities were really relevant to the academic environment,' she says. 'If a student isn't feeling comfortable to engage in specific activities, such as raising their hand in class or even attending class, then it's likely to have an outcome on academic achievement, as they're not receiving the interactions that other students are engaging in. In the US, there has been some research done in university students which showed a correlation between disturbance in body image and a lower average grade. So there does seem to be some kind of relationship between concerns around body image and not performing academically.'

It stands to reason that a child or adolescent who is thinking about their body or outward appearance has less room in their head for phonics or improper fractions or whatever they're doing in class that day, just like adults can lose brain space thinking about the way they look too. 'Generally speaking, there's research evidence to show that when adults worry about their body image it impacts their cognitive performance, and we'd expect to see this in children and adolescents too,' says Melissa. 'This is likely due to distraction and taking up that cognitive resource that would otherwise be spent on academic pursuits, and given that there's evidence in adults and university students related to some of these aspects, I think we would definitely expect this to be similar in children too. Although research is limited in children, two studies have shown that girls aged eight to eleven who are exposed to sexualised media, or who endorse dietary restraint, performed worse on cognitive tasks involving reaction time and maths.'

But how can we tell if a kid isn't engaging in class – or even turning up for class – due to the way they feel about their body, or if they're getting teased by their peers? What if the issue isn't the way they feel about their body but the way their body is being treated by other kids? Well, according to Melissa, it's two sides of the same coin. 'If someone isn't going to school and isn't engaging, whether that's due to the fear of being teased about their body or appearance, or the fear of looking bad in front of others, in one sense you could say that it doesn't matter because the outcome is the same; they're being deprived of a set of experiences that they otherwise would have. The key therefore is that we provide interventions that address body image at different levels – helping the child, as well as cultivating a positive environment.'

If we can help children to feel better in their own bodies this may have a knock-on positive impact on how they treat other bodies too.

Body image and society

Body image issues go even deeper than the way they affect children on an individual level. Your kids (and mine) don't need to be suffering with anxiety, or disordered eating, or low self-esteem, or skipping PE – or school – in order for us to care about this subject. On a wider level, body image concerns affect us all, even if we don't realise it and even if our kids aren't themselves struggling with obvious problems related to body image. Because body image isn't just an individual issue, it's a social justice issue. We need to look at the bigger picture.

The ideas, values and norms around bodies all contribute to a culture of body dissatisfaction, weight stigma and general unhappiness. These issues don't just affect children in marginalised bodies or children who are struggling with negative feelings about their bodies: they affect ALL children. A 2017 report from the World Health Organization (WHO) found that children in higher weight categories are 63 per cent more likely to get bullied than other kids.[16] So early ingrained weight bias is causing kids to be bullied, be the bully or live in fear of being bullied. Either way, it's not good.

In 2019 *The Lancet Public Health* published a report called 'Addressing Weight Stigma'.[17] This report acknowledged that discrimination based on body size even happens in the very places you might think adults and children would be safest: in GP surgeries and hospitals. The report identified weight stigma as 'the discrimination, bias and social exclusion based on someone's weight' and, interestingly, pointed to evidence that this weight stigma doesn't just affect people in bigger bodies – it affects people in smaller bodies too. The report also admitted that people in bigger bodies often say they receive poorer care, and that medical students who are a higher weight carry with them internalised weight stigma too.

And it gets worse. People are also losing out on jobs and promotions simply because of the shape of their bodies. In 2005 a study of more than 2,000 HR professionals found that a whopping 93 per cent of people questioned would choose a 'normal weight' applicant over someone in a higher weight body.[18] And 30 per cent of the people questioned also believed 'obesity is a valid medical reason for not employing a person', while a further 15 per cent agreed they'd be 'less likely to promote an obese employee'.

Weight stigma is a widely recognised problem, with respected medical journals publishing on it and even the European Court of Justice ruling on it. But take one look at Twitter, or the news, or even some of the most popular shows on the BBC and Netflix, and you'd be forgiven for thinking weight-based discrimination is totally acceptable – funny, even. As I write this the UK is a few months into the COVID-19 pandemic and the Internet memes of pre- and post-'quarantine bodies' are rife. Bodies, it seems, are still the punchline, and weight stigma is getting the last laugh.

And all the while, little ears are listening. Children are not only being treated differently because of the shape of their bodies but they're growing up in a culture that normalises weight stigma and discrimination, being exposed to these messages and ideas every day in some of the places they should be safest, learning to value themselves and others based on the shape of their bodies. It's no wonder some children as young as three feel bad about their bodies; it's more of a wonder that age isn't even younger.

Professor Heather Widdows is a professor of philosophy at the University of Birmingham and author of *Perfect Me: Beauty as an Ethical Ideal*. Through the #EverydayLookism campaign, Heather's working to end appearance-based discrimination, which she says affects us on both an individual and a societal level. And when it comes to the societal cost, she says there are various layers to the problem: 'Individual harms can become cumulative and add up. The more you put your sense of identity in your "appearance piece of pie", the less happy you're able to be, and that has knock-on effects for what else you can do. So in a way those are individual harms of the global beauty ideal, but collectively that's a serious amount of our young people and our future who are not focusing on increasing their intellectual abilities, their capacities, their emotional range, and are just focusing on their appearance.'

Heather argues that this has a bigger knock-on effect for global society too: 'If you put together the diet and exercise trade, with the make-up trade and the fashion trade, you're probably doing far more than most GDPs of very small countries – and more than the arms or drugs trade. What would we do with that money if we didn't do this? These are basic justice questions. What is legitimate to do with money when we don't cure illnesses like malaria or TB, and when we've still got very much of the world living on the poverty line?' The impact of appearance-based insecurities is something that we need to take more seriously, says Heather, and there's no time to lose.

'If you think about just how much of an impact body image anxiety has, the mental health capacities on young people and the way it prevents them from doing other things – to study, to focus, to want to speak out on important issues – if this was a new drug or some video game making our kids so unable to do things and eating into their time, then we would be acting on it as a public health issue.'

HOPE

It's normal to feel bad about your body though, right? Especially when you consider that there are more than 43 million people in the UK on a diet[19] and, in 2018 alone, more than 28,000 cosmetic procedures took place here.[20] So, as parents, aren't we just fighting a losing battle? Well, no, actually. Because while the number of people requesting surgical fixes and embarking on diet regimes may be on the rise, there's also a growing number of people opting out altogether.

From body image therapists to body-positive activists, educators teaching about body image in school PSHE lessons and campaigners calling for changes to the way weight-loss products are advertised and eating disorders are diagnosed, there is an increasing number of people who refuse to buy into the multibillion-pound body-transformation industry. They argue there's another way; that negative body image is not inevitable.

And this is good news for the next generation of dieters and cosmetic surgery volunteers (i.e. our children).

If you're reading this book then you are part of the solution. Experts say parents and the trusted adults around children can play a huge role in helping kids feel good about their bodies. And we can also play an important role in calling out some of the prejudices and discrimination that may be adding to the appearance-based values our kids are internalising without us even being aware (again, this book will help with that). Because if these prejudices didn't exist, it's likely many children wouldn't be struggling with body image issues at all. As Nadia Craddock said earlier, many body insecurities are based on people not feeling they match up to whatever body ideal is 'in vogue' at the time. Get rid of the ideal and you get rid of 99.9 per cent of the problem.

I can see you rolling your eyes. I know this is probably an impossible task. But while we might not lose these unattainable standards and overhaul our society's appearance-obsessed culture altogether, we can at least teach our kids to be a bit kinder to themselves when they don't meet (or feel like they don't meet) the ideal. And we can continue to chip away at challenging the ideas that make us and our children feel bad in the first place. In a society where it's normal to feel bad about your body, it's a radical act to love it.

It stands to reason that raising body happy kids is a big step towards raising children who are confident, have a strong sense of their own worth, are less likely to suffer from health issues related to poor body image and less likely to buy into cultural ideas that discriminate against people for the way they look. So how do we get there? It might not be as hard as you think, and with this book in your hands you're already halfway there.

The first step towards raising body happy children is in what we *don't* do. And that starts with saying no to diet culture.

BODY HAPPY KIDS TOOLKIT

Affirmations

The science

Affirmations aren't just woo-woo nonsense. There's a whole lot of evidence to show they actually work. Positive affirmations are based on a psychological theory called Self-Affirmation Theory, which says we keep up a global narrative about ourselves called our self-identity, but this narrative is not strictly defined. This is good news because it suggests we can boost certain parts of our self-identity by working on how we speak to ourselves every day.

There's lots of neuroscientific research based on this theory, with scientists getting into the nitty-gritty of our brains to see what happens when we practise self-affirmation tasks. What's more, various studies have found that self-affirmations can even reverse the negative impact of seeing media-perfect bodies.[21] Not only can affirmations give us a good grounding and resilience to buffer some of the toxic body messages out there in the real world, they can reverse some of the damage entirely. This is all backed by a psychology treatment approach called cognitive behavioural therapy (CBT), which is based on experiments that prove it's possible to reframe our thought processes and create new mental patterns entirely by changing the way we think. It's literally mind-blowing.

There's also scientific evidence to show that it's not only the way we speak to ourselves which affects how we feel about our bodies – we're also affected by the way others speak to themselves too. A 2018 study found that children who are exposed to negative body talk are less likely to eat mindfully or appreciate their bodies.[22] So this exercise focuses on evidence based around the positive effect of affirmations as well as the research showing the damaging impact of body shaming yourself in front of your kids.

I'm not suggesting that you will fix all your body insecurities or heal your child's growing negative body image by just standing in front of the mirror and saying 'I am beautiful'. But there is merit in really examining the way you speak to yourself – and then understanding how this can affect your child. As well as the 2018 study, there's lots of other evidence to show children learn through role modelling, so if they see you standing in front of the mirror every day pulling at your clothes or talking in a negative way about your own body, research shows this can have a really damaging impact on your own child's body image.[23]

The tool: a daily body love exercise

You can use the following activity for all children – from toddlers to teens – and you might even find it helps you feel better about your own body too. I've included a few simple tweaks you might want to make depending on the age of your child, and there are many ways you can develop the activity to keep it interesting and make it easy to incorporate into your daily routine.

Mirror, mirror on the wall

Encourage your child to look in the mirror and point out one thing they love. This is something you can get involved in too. Changing the language you use from negative to positive and moving the focus from how your body *looks* to what it can *do* is a great way to role model positive body image. For example, switch 'I hate my arms and how this top looks on me' to 'I love how strong my arms are and how they give you brilliant hugs'. Ask your child to give you an example of something they like about their own body too – and try to keep the focus on how their body functions instead of its appearance.

Consistency is key

This doesn't have to be a formal exercise that takes up hours of every day. It could just be a quick two minutes as you get your child ready for school in the morning. Evidence shows that consistency is key, so repeating it regularly with your kids will really make a difference.

Take it away from appearance

Affirmations which focus on what your body can do over what it looks like are a great way to start building resilience and teach your child that their body is not a decorative object, and it is not where their value in the world lies. Here are some brilliant affirmations you can write down and practise daily with your child, while looking in the mirror:

- » 'I am strong.'
- » 'My body is my own.'
- » 'I am enough, just as I am.'
- » 'My body can do amazing things.'

my Body IS MY OWN

There are various ways you can tweak this exercise to develop it into an engaging activity for your kids. Here are some ideas:

Ages 0–3: Add these words to the tune of your child's favourite nursery rhyme and sing them together.

Ages 3–5: Ask your child to repeat each affirmation and draw a picture of what it looks like. Or print the affirmations out and ask your child to colour the letters in.

Age 5–8: If your child is learning to read, you can use this as an opportunity to practise together. If your child is learning to write, you could ask them to copy the letters and write them down themselves, before repeating them back to you. If your child is already reading and writing, you could ask them to write some sentences that include the words in the affirmation. For example, 'I am strong when I ... ' Or you could encourage them to write a 'self-love' letter to themselves that feature some of the affirmations.

Age 8–12: Use the affirmations as a starter for a storytelling activity. Ask your child to tell you a story about when they last felt strong, for example.

Teenagers: Use a free online graphic design website (see Resources, page 233) to encourage your teen to turn these sentences into affirmation cards. They can experiment with font and colour, then save the images to their computer to print off or to their phone to look at when they need a body image boost.

The benefits of this exercise are multiple. It's an opportunity to bond through a creative activity, to gently promote ideas around body autonomy and positive body attitudes to your child, and to engage in an anxiety-reducing mindfulness activity. (Art is a great way to take the focus off the body and get out of your head, which is proven to lower stress levels, with many therapists using art as a tool to lower anxiety in their patients.)

Even if you just take two things away from this toolkit – to encourage yourself and your children to speak positively about your bodies and to focus on what bodies can do over what they look like – this will have an impact on your children's body image and self-esteem in the long run.

CHAPTER 2

Diet Culture: How to Spot It and Why It's Damaging for Your Kids

The term 'diet culture' is bandied around a lot these days, but what exactly does it mean? If you don't do diets does that mean you don't need to worry about diet culture? How does diet culture affect children – and why does it all matter? This chapter will answer all of these questions, and more.

We're going to look at the history of diet culture and how it's morphed into the way it shows up today. And we're going to look at how diet culture has wound itself like a silent weed around the institutions our children should feel safest in – their doctor's surgeries, schools and the places they play.

It doesn't all make for bleak reading though, because as you read this chapter it will hopefully ignite a tiny spark of motivation to take on this colossal issue and fight it in your own home and community. And at the end of this chapter you'll be handed another set of tools on a platter to take out into the world and use in the battle (page 60). But before we can take diet culture down, we first need to shine a light on what it actually is. So let's begin.

THE SILENT THIEF

In my garden I have a weed that I wage war on year after year. Bindweed grows seemingly out of nowhere, silently wrapping itself around the other plants, choking them. With its bright white trumpet-shaped flowers it can often be mistaken for a regular plant itself, but the way it twines around other plants and smothers them is far from pretty. With every piece of bindweed that I tear out from the root another ten long tendrils appear, binding themselves to anything nearby. If I'm not vigilant it can take over whole swathes of my garden and kill everything in sight. If diet culture was a weed it would be bindweed.

Like bindweed, diet culture isn't always easy to spot and, on the surface, it can often be mistaken for something else. Just as bindweed quickly made itself at home in my garden and took over, diet culture has seeped into many areas of society and is now so normalised its roots are like a tangled web of weeds wrapped around many parts of our life, stifling it.

The fancy explanation of diet culture is that it's a system of beliefs that equates thinness with beauty, health, success and happiness. But there's a simpler way to look at it: it's a thief. Diet culture steals our time, energy, money, brain space and happiness. And on a more sinister level, it's stealing our children's childhoods.

Diet culture tells us that one type of body is better than another. It tells us that people in that type of body are more worthy of respect and kindness and compassion. And it

repeatedly plants the seed – and often blatantly shouts from the rooftops – that anyone who has a body that strays from this idea of perfection is lazy, greedy, unhealthy and a drain on society.

Diet culture tells us that parents of children in higher weight bodies are bad parents and that anyone in a bigger body, or with a child in a bigger body, looks this way because they are wilfully ignorant or just plain stupid. And all the while our children are growing up surrounded by these messages, judging themselves and other people based on these appearance-related values.

Living in diet culture is like living in a goldfish bowl, swimming around and around and around. We all live in it and we're all swimming in it, which often makes it harder to spot. It's only when you start to notice it that you're able to swim up to the surface and catch a breath – and maybe even jump out of the goldfish bowl to live on the other side of the glass.

Diet culture knows the general public is getting wise to the dangers of diets and that the blatant beauty ideals of the eighties and nineties aren't cool anymore, so it's worked hard to weave its way into conversations around health, transforming itself as the answer to how to make society healthier, solve 'the obesity epidemic' and prevent the 'drain' on healthcare resources. It's so sneaky I'd applaud it for its cleverness if it wasn't so dangerous – and if it hadn't started coming so obviously for our children.

I was born in 1983, which also happens to be when the weight-loss industry exploded. Although my parents didn't go to diet clubs or really talk about diets in front of me or my sister, I do remember one diet book on our bookshelf. Rosemary Conley's *Hip and Thigh Diet* featured long slender legs and a washboard stomach on the front cover and called itself 'the dieting revolution of the decade'. My parents had the first edition of the book, which was published in 1988, and I remember it making sporadic appearances every few years a few months before our family summer holiday, as my mum and dad made a half-hearted effort to 'get in shape'.

In many respects I was extremely lucky, because the occasional 'hip and thigh health kick' was the only time I was really exposed to diets within my family home. But despite having parents who only fell prey to the diet pressure occasionally, I was still growing up swimming in diet culture. By the age of ten I was starting to lose interest in my Sylvanian Families and colouring books and had discovered a new love of pop music. I covered my walls with pictures of Take That carefully cut out of *Top of the Pops* magazine and proudly wore my 'TT' necklace and watch to school. I remember watching the music video to 'Babe' and thinking that if Mark Owen was ever going to fall in love with me, I'd better do my best to look like the woman in the video.

A year or two later I'd swapped my Saturday morning pocket money spends on sweets for the latest issue of *Just Seventeen*, *Mizz* or *Bliss* magazine. I spent many a weekend devouring the advice columns, the fashion spreads and the beauty pages (this is where I learned the hot tip that Vaseline on your eyelashes does the same job as clear mascara and can also double as a great eye make-up remover if you can't afford the bus fare into town to go to Superdrug). These magazines, just like everything else, were a product of their time and the society that we lived in. While I learned lots of useful things in them, I also learned that 'hot bodies' tend to only look one way, and that if I was going to be the popular girl at school then that was the type of body I needed to aim for.

These ideas were confirmed by some of my favourite films, often rented on VHS from our local Blockbuster (retro!). There was *Death Becomes Her* (Goldie Hawn finds the secret to everlasting life and beauty, drinks a magic potion and loses a significant amount of weight, winning back her former husband and getting rich in the process), *Clueless* (the main character Cher has everything a teen could wish for – a revolving wardrobe, unrivalled status at school and a mansion – but apparently lives with a fear of becoming fat, calls herself a 'heifer' and often berates herself for eating) and many other films where the message was clear: this is what pretty looks like, and this is what you need to do if you want to be popular, happy and successful. And of course this was the case with most of my favourite TV shows too. Remember, this was the nineties when *Friends* was the cool show of the moment, a show that regularly wheeled out one of the cast members in a fat suit to play a formerly large version of themselves. Unlike the thin version, Fat Monica was shy, messy and less-than-capable. It didn't take a rocket scientist to understand what we were being told: when Monica lost the weight she also lost all the personality traits that had supposedly been holding her back from succeeding in life.

Just like everyone I knew, I internalised these messages. I'd panic if I went into Miss Selfridge or Tammy Girl and I didn't fit into the size I'd bought on my last shopping trip. I'd take care not to eat the leftover cookies from my weekend shift at Millie's Cookies, instead bringing a full bag into college to hand out in the canteen the next day. And I put my body under constant surveillance. While I wasn't going to diet clubs or counting calories specifically, every 'healthy eating' phase was most definitely a diet, even if I didn't name it as such. There was the one time I read about the benefits of a January detox and took my mum's credit card to Tesco, where I bought a trolley's worth of fruit and veg to create elaborate concoctions as part of a 'juice cleanse'. Yep, most definitely a diet.

My behaviour wasn't unusual though, and it was nothing to worry about from an outside perspective. I was a keen dancer and loved athletics and cross-country at school. I enjoyed food and would get excited about the meals we'd eat at Christmas, or on holiday, or on a Friday night 'takeaway night'. I was out-going and happy in the main, but I was also a teenager, which is very often never easy. And the diet culture I was swimming in, constantly reinforcing ideas of perfection, of beauty, of health, of what you needed to look like to be valued and gain success and be happy, certainly didn't help.

Twenty years later and the magazines, films and TV shows may have changed, not to mention the existence of social media (which we'll talk about later in the book), but diet culture is still very much here. We've moved on from some of the more blatant diet culture messaging around beauty and entered a new era of diet culture disguised as 'wellness'. But the message remains the same: this is what you need to look like to be healthy and, therefore, be valued, gain success and be happy. Diet culture tells us health only looks one way and that to be healthy is to be beautiful. And now there's a new cohort of potential recruits: our children.

In their 'Somebody Like Me' report of 2017, the Be Real Campaign found that 52 per cent of 11- to 16-year-olds regularly worry about the way they look.[1] That's important brain space taken up by diet culture that could be spent doing, achieving and just enjoying life without the added layer of pressure of fretting about changing bodies. And as we've already seen in Chapter 1, diet culture isn't just affecting teenagers. It's coming for children at a younger and younger age – often in the places we think they're safest.

When I founded the #FreeFromDiets movement in 2019 it was born out of a plethora of messages from parents on social media telling me that their children's schools and clubs were being used as a recruitment ground by diet clubs and weight-loss brands seeking new members. I regularly get sent pictures of school railings in the UK decorated with marketing material for some of these brands, or pictures of leaflets sent home in children's book bags. Meanwhile, as my own daughters get stuck into Disney+, Netflix or YouTube, I'm reminded of all the insidious ways diet culture is coming for them without them even realising it. And this is before they're even old enough to have an Instagram account or get lost in TikTok.

Saying no to diet culture isn't always easy, but it is necessary if we're going to raise body happy kids who love the skin they're in regardless of what they look like. And as we're often told, the first step to beating your enemy is to know it, which is where this next bit of the book comes in.

A BRIEF HISTORY OF DIET CULTURE

As we've just learned, diet culture is an oppressive system of beliefs that equates happiness, health, beauty and other forms of success with thinness. It leads to weight stigma and the discrimination and prejudice faced by people in bigger bodies every single day. Any culture that creates an ideal will mean those who are further away from the ideal are not only left out of conversations, they are actively discriminated against too.

In her book *Fearing the Black Body: The Racial Origins of Fat Phobia*, Sabrina Strings, PhD, shows how diet culture is a direct product of racism.[2] We learn about François Bernier, who lived in France in the 1600s and wrote a manifesto called 'A New Division of the Earth', segregating humans into different groups based on their appearance. The manifesto created a hierarchy of races, with white people at the top. This became the blueprint for 'race scientists' to justify colonisation, the enslavement of Black people and, later, eugenics. These so-called scientists described Black people as having 'voracious' or 'gluttonous' appetites and being 'lazy', 'simple' and 'stupid'. It was a clear way to dehumanise Black people so they could be treated as possessions rather than people.

'I believe race science may have started off as a way to justify slavery,' says Aisha Nash, who is an anti-diet yoga teacher and regularly uses her platform to educate on the racist roots of diet culture and the wellness industry. 'It evolved as a "science" at the exact same time as the Second Atlantic system, when the British and French started to enslave Africans. It was incredibly insidious, using pseudoscience such as phrenology, anthropometry and other such means to categorise humans based on their appearance.'

Any conversation about diet culture today can't ignore these racist roots of the industry, explains Aisha, because it impacts so many different areas of society. 'If we hope to create equitable access to health and wellness, we really need to discuss the way that diet culture and wellness culture are shaped by whiteness, and this idea of acting to a white standard. White people are the global minority, and yet everywhere there is this need to assimilate our lives and our eating habits into those that most resemble white culture, even when it creates distancing between us and our own culture.'

While the race scientists were sharing their views on the hierarchy of humans, the Evangelical Protestant movement saw the shape of someone's body as a signifier for how religious they were, with the assumption that people in bigger bodies were prone to committing the sin of gluttony. If you wanted to show you were a good, moral, upstanding citizen then you'd better be thin (and white). Anyone who deviated from that ideal risked being shunned by the fashionable upper social circles of society at best – or cast out to the margins of wider society. Want to be rich, popular and well-respected? Avoid 'gluttony', get on the 'temperance' wagon and make sure your corset or your waist-coat doesn't bulge in all the wrong places.

You might think none of this affects the way we see food now, but Aisha explains that two names in particular are still household ones you're likely to see in your kitchen cupboards even today. 'John Kellogg and Sylvester Graham were both temperance activists in the nineteenth century. They very much believed that people should avoid all forms of external stimulation; they hated sex, masturbation and also thought that food was much too exciting. They made their money selling plain and unstimulating wholegrain food products and would lecture humans – especially women – on the way they should look and behave, to show superiority over other humans.'

Diet culture isn't a new phenomenon then, but rather one that goes back hundreds of years. The narrative might have changed, but the idea that you can tell someone's moral worth and value just from the shape of their body is still the same.

Fast forward to 1884 and the introduction of the first public weighing scales, designed by Norfolk-born engineer Percival Everitt in the UK and swiftly taken up by all of America.[3] For the first time, Americans could easily find out how much they weighed without going to the doctor. By feeding a nickel into a slot on a machine (in just the same way as they'd later fire up a jukebox or a bubble gum dispenser) they'd be able to chart their weight. These appeared in shops and in busy shopping areas, and by 1936 the US Department of Commerce announced, 'Penny weighing scales are the principle [sic] means of 130 million people keeping in touch with their weight and health.[4] The penny weighing machines were big business and became a form of entertainment in their own right, using lots of extra gimmicks to encourage people to use them, including a free horoscope reading with your ticket or a collectible picture of a Hollywood movie star.[5] Want a fun family day out? Go shopping and weigh yourself!

Soon weight would be tied up with ideas of health (which we'll look at in more detail in the next chapter) and doctors started sharing their ideas on the ideal body type people should be striving for. Articles appeared in journals stating the dangers of being too big, although the evidence with which they asserted their claims was scant. The theme running through these texts was one of personal responsibility, and there was many a doctor ready to step in and sell a 'cure' for fatness. And so, the earliest diets were born.

Over a hundred years later and much has changed, but also, not much at all. We still value bodies based on their appearance, are terrified of being 'too big' and are told to believe that the size of our bodies is totally within our control. We might not judge people's religious character based on the shape of their bodies, but the moral judgement is definitely still there. Anyone who's ever heard it muttered that 'they've let themselves go' will have had first-hand experience of this.

These days diet culture has become deeply entrenched in ideas of what health looks like, and the cultural obsession with wellness as a trend doesn't help. You need money to go to spin classes, grab a green juice smoothie on your way to work and embark on whatever the latest clean-eating, whole-food eating, plant-based eating fad of the moment is. Glossy hair, white teeth and toned abs are just as important as the designer clothes,

Insta-worthy house and fast car in showing someone's social status and wealth. And what's more, there's an idea that anyone who looks like this isn't just healthy – they're inherently a good and responsible person too, because they're 'taking care of' and 'prioritising' their health.

Diet culture has cleverly repackaged itself up as 'wellness', but the overall message is the same as that of one, two or even three hundred years ago: to be a good, moral and upstanding citizen, on an upward social trajectory, you need to look a certain way. We've swapped religion for health, but the outcome is the same: we're still classifying people and making judgements based on their bodies.

Sarah McMahon is a psychologist and director of Body-Matters Australasia, a group offering treatment for eating disorders and body image issues, as well as advocating on social justice issues relating to these areas. 'When I'm talking about diet culture, I'm really thinking about everything that maintains the thin ideal in society,' says Sarah. 'It's all the different messages from all the different stakeholders that perpetuate the idea that thinness is the ideal. But it's very hard to see something you're immersed in and, often, it's only when you step back from it that you become more aware that it actually exists. Messages are so unclear about the relationship between thinness and health. Just because someone is thin doesn't mean they're healthy. And so many people can be engaging in really unhealthy practices to obtain a thin body, which actually compromises their health greatly.'

Now that diet culture is so tied up in health it can make it even harder for parents to say no to it. We want to do right by our kids, which often means encouraging them to 'be healthy'. And when we're told that healthy looks a certain way it's tempting to inadvertently encourage our children down the diet culture rabbit hole with us. It starts with banning biscuits and introducing a rigid exercise routine but, says Sarah, this can end with disordered eating or even – in some cases – a full-blown eating disorder. 'There's this idea that the odd anorexic is a small price to pay for the "war on obesity" and there's a notion that it doesn't really matter that there are going to be casualties against diet culture, and that the only people impacted are those with an eating disorder. But the impact is far broader. Because there are varying degrees of disordered eating in our society. Rather than having an "obesity epidemic", I think we have an epidemic of disordered eating, which is a direct result of diet culture. The dangerous thing is the volume of disorder that's peppered throughout our society without anyone having any insight into what is happening. And these people are experiencing varying degrees of body shame and body anxiety, which has a severe impact on their quality of life.'

As we heard in Chapter 1, all body ideals are bad news for body image, and this is something Sarah sees time and again with the patients she treats at her practice. 'Many adults have grown up with the belief that if you're fat you can't fall in love or have a partner,' says Sarah. 'These ideas are things people are absolutely wedded to because there's such a confirmation bias. People have had a lifetime of it being confirmed to them that their beliefs are true.'

Diet culture won't let us go without a fight though. The way it's shape-shifted and morphed into different areas over the many years might make it hard to spot, but ultimately the idea is simple: if it's telling you that your body is wrong, or the body of your child is wrong, then it's probably diet culture.

So why does diet culture do this? Why is it so important for us to feel like our bodies are wrong? And what does diet culture gain from making our kids think their bodies are wrong too? Well, unsurprisingly, it's all about the money.

DIET CULTURE IS BIG BUSINESS

Since diet culture has managed to wrap itself around ideas of health, it's often seen as a public service provider, or even a charity. In the UK, diet companies have links with the National Health Service, and doctors and other health professionals are often encouraged to refer patients to these groups in the NHS 'Making Every Contact Count' approach to behaviour change. This can make it really confusing for parents, because on the one hand they want their kids to be confident and feel good in their bodies, but on the other hand they're being told the route to their children finding health and happiness (and feeling good in their skin) is to change their bodies, which, as we've already heard, is a damaging message on many levels.

There's one important thing to remember in all of this though, and that is that diet culture is big business. There are many companies profiting from all the people who want to change their bodies (either for beauty or health reasons). Diet culture is making a lot of people a lot of money. It's not a charity. It's not a public service provider. And, ultimately, it serves the diet industry's financial interests for all of us to live with constant body blues.

The global weight management market was worth an estimated $189.8 billion in 2018 and has been projected to reach anything from $270 to $422 billion by 2025.[6] Either way, that's a lot of money. In the UK, the two leading diet brands have programmes for children as young as 11 and 13 respectively, which kids can access as long as they're accompanied by someone in their family who is also a member and, in some cases, are referred by a doctor – so this isn't just an industry aimed at adults.[7] And over in the US, in 2019 WW launched a weight-loss app for children as young as eight years old.[8] At the time, various publications noted the app could be a savvy move for a company looking to expand their customer base.[9] It makes good business sense to recruit the next generation of dieters, and persuading parents that it's in their children's best interests to jump on the diet bandwagon in the name of health is a genius marketing strategy.

However, the reality is that the stats don't back up what the diet industry claims. You've probably heard it before, but diets really don't work. An analysis of 29 weight-loss studies found that 77 per cent of the participants regained the weight they'd lost after five years.[10] But in her book *Just Eat It*, Laura Thomas, PhD, warns the figure is probably higher, writing, 'we don't publish weight-loss studies where people don't lose weight, so the finding that participants regain 77% of their initial weight is likely to be higher!'[11] Thomas also points to a 2017 analysis study to find out how 'successful' people are when they do diets at home (as opposed to the controlled environment of a clinical trial).[12] The study found that 'almost 60% of people who started a commercial weight-loss program were unable to meet their target weight-loss goal of 5%'.

Diet culture is clever though, because it makes us believe it's our fault for either not losing the weight or for putting it back on, so we try again with a hardened resolve. Or we try another diet. And so the cycle continues and, importantly for the diet industry, we spend more money.

Christy Harrison is an anti-diet registered dietician, a certified intuitive eating counsellor and author of the book *Anti-Diet*. She also hosts *Food Psych*, one of the leading podcasts about this subject. 'The diet industry thrives on people coming back for more and thinking they didn't have enough willpower or they have to work harder,' says Christy. 'Diet companies and a lot of the medical industrial complex that pushes people to lose weight are just part of this larger system.'

The aggressive marketing towards children disguised as health concern is an area of real danger according to Christy and many dieticians and nutritionists like her. 'It's interesting because over the years people have started to get wise to diets and to realise they don't work, and so diet culture and the diet industry has shape-shifted into what I call the Wellness Diet – the sneaky, modern guise of diet culture that pretends it's not a diet, it's a lifestyle. We're told it's not about aesthetics, it's about well-being. But in the last five years or so there's been a strong movement towards body positivity and giving up dieting, and I think the diet industry is really running scared with that because it's cutting into their market share and threatening their bottom line.'

The way diet culture has wrapped itself around ideas of health is a clever way for it to target children, because while parents will often be on board with protecting their kids from narrow beauty ideals, ultimately we want what's best for our kids and so we see helping them to 'be healthy' as a positive thing – even if that means going on a diet (whether it's via a shiny new kid-friendly app or joining up to a friendly weekly meeting).

'It's a bit like how cigarettes were given to soldiers in World War Two to get them hooked and create new customers for life,' says Christy. 'The diet industry is minting customers while they're young to get them signed up for life. It's really insidious because parents want to do right for their kids; they want their kids to be healthy and have the best possible outcomes in terms of physical health. But unfortunately, unbeknownst to the parents, that's at the expense of their kids' mental health and well-being, and it's also at the expense of their physical health too.'

We'll discuss what health actually is and why we need to move away from the diet culture definition of health in the next chapter, but no modern-day discussion of diet culture can ignore the way it's wrapped itself up in and tied itself around what we understand health to be today.

Many diet companies encourage parents to bring their children along to meetings, advertising themselves as safe spaces for kids. In my conversations with many people who go to these groups they tell me they are an important source of community and social contact, a highlight of their week. In making their groups 'family-friendly' the companies hit two birds with one stone: they get more customers through the door and they get an opportunity to engage with potential future recruits (children). And by positioning themselves in this way – as a family-friendly 'lifestyle', approved by doctors, part of the community and as a public service – it means we lose sight of the sole aim of the industry: to make money.

This isn't to say that everyone who works for these companies is in on the secret, or that everyone who goes to these meetings doesn't feel helped or find an important sense of community. But it's important to look at the overall picture and be aware of the other perspective: that this is a business that lots of people are profiting from, and it's potentially causing many levels of harm for our children.

Away from the diet and weight-loss industry is another growing business that relies on us not liking our bodies. The global cosmetic surgery procedures market is anticipated to reach $50.5 billion by 2027, and it's safe to say that if we all felt good about our bodies and didn't want to change them, this would be a death knell for the industry.[13] Between 2017 and 2019 more than 26,000 women had cosmetic surgery in the UK, compared to 2,304 men.[14] Current law in the UK states that anyone over the age of 16 can have cosmetic surgery, and although it's recommended that they get parental consent, this isn't a legal requirement.

It's all part of a bigger picture: capitalism.

If we all liked our bodies, and our kids were growing up liking their bodies, then we would not be spending billions and billions of pounds trying to 'fix' them. Our poor body image might not be good for us, but it sure is brilliant for the economy.

HOW DIET CULTURE IMPACTS KIDS

Go back to that first moment when you thought your body was a problem and think about where this thought came from. For many people, this thought will have arrived before they reached adulthood. It might even have arrived so early on in childhood you can't remember when exactly it hit. My own teen adolescent angst over small boobs, big shoulders and a need to keep my tummy in check arrived fairly late. This is largely because of my privilege as a white, nondisabled, thin child who identified with the gender I'd been assigned at birth. Because of diet culture and the way our society is set up to favour certain types of bodies over others, many children are experiencing concerns over their bodies at a far younger age, before they are anywhere near adolescence.

We've already heard how body image issues can impact children on an individual level, and we've also heard how body ideals that exist in society can create the body image problems in the first place. We've also heard how diet culture has its roots in racism, and how it's seeped into ableist ideas of what it means (and looks like) to be healthy. These oppressive belief systems are affecting all children in all bodies, and if we care about helping the kids in our life to feel good in their skin, we need to be aware that diet culture is directly at odds with this mission.

In their 'Girls' Attitudes Survey' of 2019, Girlguiding UK found that 25 per cent of seven- to ten-year-old girls surveyed had been bullied for the way they look,[15] while a 2016 study by the advertising think tank Credos found that 55 per cent of eight- to eighteen-year-old boys would consider changing their diet to 'look better'.[16] It's safe to assume both these stats would be significantly lower – if not non-existent – if diet culture didn't exist.

It's useful to know that dieting isn't just bad for our mental health, it's bad for our physical health too. Here's Christy Harrison again: 'There's considerable research showing that weight cycling – that yo-yo of weight loss and regain – is actually independently bad for people's health and is a risk factor for things that get blamed on weight itself, like heart disease, mortality and some forms of cancer. But they can likely be explained at least in part – if not entirely – by weight cycling, and also by weight stigma, which we know is another independent risk factor for health outcomes that get blamed on weight.'

This might make for depressing reading, but it's not all bad news. While diet culture seeps into every area of life, even in some of the spaces our children should be safest, the role of parents, caregivers and key figures in kids' lives shouldn't be underestimated. Our children may be the tiny tadpoles swimming through diet culture, but with our help we can smash the glass and get them on to the other side of the diet culture goldfish bowl. And luckily for us, there are many organisations, activists and educators ready with their metaphorical hammers to help us smash the glass.

The good news

'The US weight loss industry is now worth a record $72 billion' trumpets a 2019 article by Marketdata LLC in *Business Wire*, 'but the number of dieters has fallen due to the growth of the size acceptance and body positivity movement'.[17] Diet culture is still raking it in, but the number of people aware of the dangers of dieting – and the existence of diet culture at all – is on the rise.

At the time of writing, the UK-based creator and author of *Body Positive Power*, Megan Jayne Crabbe (aka @bodyposipanda), has 1.3 million followers on Instagram, with her posts on body image, self-care, mental health and social justice issues regularly garnering in excess of 50,000 likes.[18] We'll talk about the impact of social media on kids' body image in Chapter 7, but it's useful to note here that it's played a big role in challenging some of the ideals regularly promoted by diet culture.

Celebrities such as Demi Lovato and Jameela Jamil are joining the conversation too, hitting back at narrow body ideals that are enslaving their millions of followers – many of whom are kids. In September 2019 Demi Lovato posted a photo of herself in a bikini with the accompanying caption sharing some very real talk about her previous battles with dieting. In the caption Demi celebrated her natural figure and cellulite and talked about the freedom she's felt since giving up the diet mentality.[19] The post got more than 10 million likes and counting.

These conversations are not confined to Instagram or to a corner of the Internet. In her 2020 *Rolling Stone* cover interview with Brittany Spanos, three-time Grammy award-winning singer Lizzo shared some candid thoughts on her rise to fame and her experiences as a fat Black woman in a space largely dominated by thin white women.[20] She talked about coming to terms with body dysmorphia and what the body positive movement means to her, as well as asserting that she is so much more than her body. This is a far cry from the types of conversations served up by the popular culture of the eighties and nineties that I grew up in.

Although diet culture is everywhere, still dominating many of the headlines around health, and there is still a huge amount of work to be done, little by little, it's being chipped away at. In 2019 Instagram announced it would be restricting posts that promote weight-loss and cosmetic procedures to under 18-year-olds and it would be removing posts that make 'miraculous claims' about certain diets or weight-loss products.[21] The diet teas so regularly endorsed by influencers and celebrities haven't gone away, but the fact that they can no longer be so blatantly advertised to children – or any of us – on Instagram is a step in the right direction.

As diet culture tries to invade the spaces in which our children should be safest, there's also work being done to stop it infiltrating these places. The Dove Self-Esteem Project's educational programmes are on course to help a quarter of a billion young people around the world by 2030,[22] and the Be Real Campaign, founded by YMCA and Dove,[23] has a body confidence toolkit which is being used by schools up and down the

UK. And I know from my campaign work creating workshops for teachers and youth leaders that the appetite to create body happy environments for children is huge. We might not always be able to spot diet culture, but we're starting to wake up to the fact that we no longer have to live with it. It might not always feel like it, but change is happening. And the toolkit below will help to empower you to become part of that change.

BODY HAPPY KIDS TOOLKIT
How to Cancel Diet Culture around Kids

The science

We've established the roots of diet culture − that it's not only at odds with raising body happy kids but it's actively trying to make them feel bad (while disguising itself as having their best interests at heart) − so now we need to work on spotting it.

Cognitive psychologists describe problem-solving as the mental process that people go through to discover, analyse and solve problems, and they say 'perceptually recognising' a problem is the first step to solving it. Researchers refer to the 'problem-solving cycle' and − surprise, surprise − step one is 'identifying the problem' (before 'defining the problem' and 'forming a strategy').[24]

This toolkit is based on this first step in the cognitive psychology model of problem-solving. Namely: it will help you identify the problem. This might sound easy on the surface, but because diet culture shape-shifts so often, is so normalised and often comes pretending to be 'good' for us and our kids, this is often easier said than done.

It is now so intrinsically tied up in ideas of health and wellness we can find ourselves elbow-deep in diet culture and the diet mentality, bringing our kids along for the ride, before we even realise. I imagine it's a bit like finding yourself at the top of Expedition Everest at Disney World, looking down a 60-metre drop when you'd innocently thought you'd got on the carousel for toddlers. And, just like you wouldn't easily be able to hop off the roller coaster halfway round, the same is true of diet culture.

It's all very well for me to tell you the history of diet culture and why it's a Bad Thing, but it's quite another thing being able to actively opt out of it. I'll be honest with you: opting out of diet culture is my actual job and even I can still find myself in its clutches. And if this is my job, and I'm a fully grown adult with an awareness of what diet culture is, imagine how hard it is for kids. That's why it's up to us as their trusted adults to do the work for them – to learn how to spot diet culture ourselves, so we can help the children in our life avoid its vice-like grip.

Hopefully with this tool you will be able to go some way to spotting diet culture in some of its more obvious, as well as its more insidious, forms.

The tool: the diet culture tick sheet

This list of questions will help you spot diet culture around kids, with some suggestions for ways to counteract it when you do. If the answer to any of the questions is 'yes' then it's diet culture (even if it pretends it isn't). This isn't an exhaustive list and, because we know diet culture is a shape-shifting genius, we need to be mindful that by tomorrow it might have found a new form that we need to be vigilant to. But having this in mind and using these questions as a starting point will help you be more aware of some of the more insidious ways in which it can present and what you can do to help your kids when it does.

My suggestion for every one of these points is that if you see diet culture, call it out. Talk to your children about it, help them learn the skills to start questioning what they see or hear, so they can challenge the status quo. We're not just raising kids who feel better about their bodies, we're raising mini activists who can continue to create change for future generations.

☑ Are there before and after pictures?

Whether it's a magazine article about a 'weight-loss transform-ation' or an advert outside a local gym, before and after pictures are common – and children see them just as regularly as adults.

Introduce the idea that all bodies are good bodies, and you can't tell much about someone from the shape of their body. Discuss the idea that sometimes businesses use these images to try to encourage people to spend their money, because these photos are designed to make them feel like their bodies are 'wrong' and that spending their money will make their bodies 'right'. For older children, you can talk about some of the ways the before and after photos are different, that have nothing to do with the body. For example, is the lighting different in both photos? Does the person have a different hairstyle? Are they smiling in one and not the other? This will help them learn some media literacy skills (which we'll delve deeper into later in the book) to help untangle what some of these images are trying to convey.

☑ Is one type of body being presented as better than another?

Is this type of body presented as stronger, fitter, healthier or more beautiful? Is the person in this body shown as being happier, more successful, more popular?

Show your child some examples of people they may not see represented in their favourite YouTube channels, TV shows and magazines. Talk about plus-size athletes and Paralympians, for example, who are achieving amazing things but may not look like the person in the diet culture-infused picture. For older children, discuss the idea (without naming methods) that sometimes people do unhealthy things to make their bodies look like that, and these things can mean they end up being unwell. Seek out accounts on social media that talk about the editing and tips and tricks that some photographers, producers and content creators use to make photos look the way they do. (Although take care to avoid accounts that perpetuate body ideals by offering tutorials on how to make bodies 'look better' in photos!)

☑ Is there moralistic language around food?

Does it use words such as 'clean' or 'cleanse', 'guilt-free', 'naughty', 'cheat' or 'bad'?

Check out the tool at the end of Chapter 5 (see page 142) for ways to promote positive, joyful and healthy relationships with food. But, essentially, beware any language that imbues food with moral value. Consider talking about food as being more or less 'nutrient dense' instead of simply 'healthy' or 'unhealthy'. Instead of morally loaded words, use neutral language, and call the moral words out for what they are: diet culture. Talk to your kids about the energy that food can give you and the joy that we get from eating certain foods at times of celebration. For older kids, discuss the idea that food can be a way to bring people together – an important feature of many celebrations – and that equating cake or whatever as 'naughty' is a way to try to make us think the people who eat those foods are naughty too, when this just isn't true.

☑ When it comes to exercise, does it talk about 'burning fat', 'earning treats', 'toning your abs' or 'building muscle'?

Discuss how exercise has other benefits and can enhance your life in a way that has nothing to do with changing the appearance of your body. (Check out Chapter 6 – page 147 – for more on this.) Show your kids pictures of athletes who don't fit the thin, ripped, muscular global beauty ideal to show that you don't have to have a body like that in order to enjoy movement and achieve in sport.

☑ Does it leave out types of bodies that don't look like the thin ideal?

Many brands, producers and editors have woken up to the importance of diversity, but in a bid to 'tick the boxes' they may not be truly intersectional in their representation. They may have diversity of skin colour in their image or brand campaign or kids' storybook, for example, but not have a diversity of body shapes. They may have a disabled person, but not a disabled person in a bigger body. If this is the case, this is a chance to talk to children again about the range of different body types that exist, and to look for this representation elsewhere. It may be seeking accounts on social media that you can show your children or making a conscious effort to include a more diverse range of books on your child's bookshelf or on your borrow list from the library. The point is that the more opportunities we give children to see images that they may relate to, as well as images of people who don't look like them, the better chance we have of not just calling out diet culture but raising a generation who will cancel it completely.

CHAPTER 3

Let's Talk About Health (It's Complicated)

Before we cover any more ground, we need to address the 'But what about health?' question, which is often the main argument against body acceptance and something you might be thinking right now as you're reading this. There's an assumption that if we accept our bodies as they are, we will 'give up' on our health. So this chapter is going to look at what health is, how we define it, why poor body image is bad for health and why as adults we need to take a new approach if we care about the health of the children in our care.

I have enlisted the help of doctors, scientists and other experts, along with the results of many different studies, to help show that health and body image are intrinsically linked and that helping your kids feel good about their bodies will have a positive impact on their overall health.

We're going to hear how self-care is an important aspect of health, and how mental and physical health can't be separated. We'll also learn how teaching children to connect with their bodies will lead them to be healthier and make healthy choices as they grow up.

The ideas and the toolkit in this chapter will give you a new perspective on health that will help you separate your children's health from the way their bodies look. It will give you inspiration for ways to incorporate healthy habits into your kids' lives that have nothing to do with counting calories, because your childrens' health is not just impacted by what they eat or how much they move their bodies.

BUT WHAT ABOUT HEALTH?

People will often be on board with the idea that kids should be allowed to like their bodies ... until the 'but'. It often goes like this: 'It's all very well telling people to love their bodies and opt out of diet culture ... but what about health? At what point is it unhealthy to love your body as it is? What about the obesity epidemic?'

And I get it. I really do. We have been conditioned for years – YEARS – to believe that health is a look, something to be attained, a holy grail of enlightenment to follow with a smaller number on the scale or toned abs or a narrower waist at the end of the journey. This stuff runs deep, especially when it has come from a doctor or a trusted health professional, or a letter in your child's book bag after they were weighed at school.

While many people can get behind the idea that cellulite is normal, and that we don't all need to look like Kate Moss or one of the Kardashians, there is still a common perception that this self-acceptance is only allowed up to a certain size, at which point shrinking our kids' body is not about beauty – it's about health. The problem with this idea is that it still assumes that health is a look, measurable by size, and that we have total control over things like weight, but the truth is far more complex.

When I was growing up I had a clear idea of what 'being healthy' meant – and it was always tied up with what I believed 'being healthy' looked like. I would tell myself I was 'being healthy', but cutting past all the wellness rhetoric, the ultimate aim of the game was to shrink, tone up, be smaller. I tried all sorts of things in my quest for health and, looking back, most of those things weren't very healthy at all. They all involved intense restriction and pushing my body to its limits in a damaging way, often at times when it was most in need of gentle care (like recovering after having a baby). And how did I measure the success of each 'health mission'? I stood on the scales.

When my eldest daughter was a toddler I was working as a radio presenter doing a breakfast show. This was the same time regular fasting was the craze. During this phase I lived at least two or three days a week on a very low number of calories. This would be a tiny amount of calories on a normal day, but considering I was getting up for work at 3.30am, working and running around after a toddler all day before going to bed at 11pm, it's pretty unbelievable I didn't pass out. But everyone else in the office was doing it too, along with loads of my friends and most of the celebrities I was talking about on the radio, so I didn't even question its impact on my health. I didn't think I was 'doing a diet'; I thought I was 'being healthy'.

Theoretically, I knew diets weren't that great, but what I didn't realise was that, although I wasn't offering up my body to be weighed in a village hall as part of a diet club, I was still very much opting into diet culture. My quest for health had nothing to do with health at all. Ironically, my quest for health was leading me to do *un*healthy things.

But the problem was my unhealthy behaviour was totally normalised by the culture we live in, which tells us that health looks a certain way, and that people in bigger bodies are automatically unhealthy, and that it is our duty as responsible moral citizens to follow a 'healthy lifestyle', which is almost always about restriction and shrinking our bodies.

Let's talk about 'healthism'

In 1980 the political economist Robert Crawford coined the term 'healthism'.[1] Crawford argued that healthism meant it was no longer enough just to look healthy, we had to 'perform' being healthy too.

Healthism makes a person's health all their own responsibility, offering 'fixes' to their health at that level too. According to Crawford, as long as we view health in this way then politicians are let off the hook because we see any issue with our health as all on us, and nothing to do with the way society is set up.

Healthism directly impacts children because it sees them internalise ideas about what it means to be healthy – and what being healthy looks like. And when these ideas are thinly veiled body ideals, this can impact their body image and create problems on a bigger societal scale too.

In a 2010 paper looking at teenage girls' attitudes to health, researchers in Australia found that healthism was obvious from the way the girls spoke about PE, fitness, health and their bodies.[2] They talked about health and fitness as being an important way to control their body shape and stick to feminine appearance ideals. Meanwhile, over in Norway, researchers in 2016 interviewed a bunch of middle-aged men and found that they talked about health in terms of their body's functionality, an absence of illness, overall well-being and the importance of community and interactions with friends.[3] Those are two distinct versions of what it means to be healthy, and the version most potentially damaging to overall health and body image is the one held by the young girls.

The guys in Norway had it right: when we look at our kids' health we don't just need to think about what they're eating and how much exercise they're doing, we also need to think about how much they see their friends, how involved they are with their community and what their overall happiness and sense of well-being is.

So where did the young girls in Australia get their ideas of health from? You could argue that these alternative attitudes to health are down to cultural differences, but it could also be because diet culture has more to gain by targeting young kids (i.e. future consumers) than middle-aged men, and that making health all about body shape and driving this message home through health education initiatives predicated on the notion of health as 'a look' is another genius diet culture tactic to target kids.

The key to beating diet culture is often to take a step back and look at the bigger picture. And this is also the key to understanding the complex, multi-layered subject of health.

Let's talk about BMI

Before we go on, we need to take a closer look at where our idea of what health *looks* like has come from. What if I told you that notions of a 'normal body size' were not borne out of medical science at all, but from insurance companies? Buckle up for a quick history lesson – it's unlikely you'll have heard this one in school.

We're going back to the late 1800s when TB and pneumonia were the number one killers in America. It was a similar story back in the UK, but it's the US where we're going right now because this is where the Association of Life Insurance Medical Directors of America (ALIMDA) met for their annual meeting in 1897. It was at this meeting that the first proper standard height and weight table was presented, which was an attempt to easily define a person's health status to help insurers decide whether to grant someone health insurance.

Insurers thought that being 'underweight' put people more at risk of TB and pneumonia (making them an unsafe bet for insurance) while being 'overweight' gave them some protection against the nation's biggest killers. These tables were based on the data from 74,162 accepted life insurance applicants – who were pretty much all white middle-aged men. This model became the industry standard, later morphing into 'ideal' or 'desirable' weights as seen in the MetLife tables (named after the Metropolitan Life Insurance Company, who created them). These tables were headed up by a maths whizz called Louis Israel Dublin, who had a degree in maths and a doctorate in biology but was not a medical doctor; he was a statistician who worked for an insurance company.

Although we no longer talk about the MetLife tables, it's important to know that these were the early model for BMI, which came along a little later and is now used to define 'normal'.

BMI is a maths equation which divides your weight in kilograms by your height in metres squared. You then get a number which will sit on a scale of 'underweight' to 'obese'. When Belgian-born statistician Adolphe Quetelet (another maths whizz) came up with the index that BMI is based on, as a way to measure populational weight in 1832, he probably didn't imagine it would be used 200 years later to persuade parents to worry about their kids' weight. Fast forward to 1980 and a famous physiologist called Ancel Keys, who was a vocal hater of those MetLife tables, argued to bring back the Quetelet Index on the basis that, although 'not fully satisfactory', this index – which he rebranded as Body Mass Index (or BMI) – was better than the alternative.[4]

Whether you agree that body size is a useful indicator of health or not, there are some things you should know about BMI. Firstly, it doesn't discriminate between weight from fat and weight from 'lean mass' (that's 'muscle' to you and me). Secondly, many experts say that BMI has never been a perfect index for children. This is because children have different body compositions to adults and BMI doesn't take into consideration changes in growth patterns of kids, so on the BMI scale taller children can sometimes come out with a higher BMI.[5] What's more, evidence shows Black children often come out with overestimated BMI scores while children of South Asian heritage often come out with underestimated scores.[6]

Toral Shah is a nutritional scientist, certified functional medicine practitioner and founder of The Urban Kitchen platform. 'We have to remember that when BMI was brought in originally we didn't have computers, so it was a quick and easy way to measure populational health,' explains Toral. 'But we're now using it to measure individuals and that doesn't make sense because everyone is different. BMI doesn't take into account differences between gender or ethnicity.

It also doesn't take into context our body composition, which includes our bone density or muscle mass. Fat impacts the body physiologically in a different way to muscle, but BMI doesn't account for this. It gives no indication of someone's metabolic health at all.'

Even if you do use BMI as a scale of individual health, you need to be aware that the scale itself probably won't apply to you or your kids, says Toral. 'There's no logic or reasoning for using BMI as a measure of individual health. It's arbitrary and based on those early MetLife tables. But how can tables based on the measurements of white men possibly be an accurate measure of health for everyone? Health has become reductionist, and that's the problem. Our life and our body's biology are not that simple. It's far more complex.'

Simplifying health in this way creates huge problems, says Toral, both on an individual and societal level. 'It's time for us to move forward and personalise medicine and health. This will take some investment, but it will also save a lot of money and save a lot of people with health conditions. Unfortunately though, when we have policies made by people who don't understand health, then it's going to be very hard to change things.'

Many scientists are calling for new ways to measure weight and define 'healthy' and 'unhealthy', as they move to wage war on fat. But perhaps now is a good time to examine how unhealthy fat actually is, because we might not have the full story.

Let's talk about fat

Over the years many researchers whose work hasn't vilified fat have been the subject of derision from the medical and scientific community. George Burr is one such researcher. In 1929 he published a study which proved dietary fat was important for health – and he was rewarded with a letter of condolence for his efforts.[7]

In the late 1990s a doctor called Carl Lavie discovered that people with a higher BMI and higher fat seemed to live longer after a heart attack. His study got rejected by four major journals that refused to publish it, such was the bias against the positive role of fat.[8]

This was also the experience of Katherine Flegal, a well-respected epidemiologist from the Centers for Disease Control and Prevention in America, who'd been investigating the link between weight and health for over two decades. In 2013 Flegal reviewed 97 studies over a 15-year period from 1997 to look at the relationship between 'overweight and obesity' and mortality.[9] She found that 'overweight' people had a 6 per cent lower risk of death than those in the 'normal' weight categories, while the people in the 'mild to moderate obesity' category had the same risk as those in the 'normal' weight categories. Her findings ruffled a few feathers. One professor from Harvard was so cross he called the study 'a pile of rubbish', saying 'no one should waste their time reading it'. While many researchers now accept the results of the study, the controversy surrounding it was so ferocious it's become part of what Flegal is known for aside from the study itself – her Wikipedia page even mentions it.[10]

Before they've even begun, researchers are under pressure to find that fat = bad. And history shows that if they don't, they face scorn, derision and intense criticism. When we hear about the dangers of fat, what the headlines often fail to tell us is that there is a difference between correlation and causation. It is often not as simple as 'being fat causes disease' because this doesn't account for the missing piece of the puzzle.

If we're not measuring health by BMI or weight or anything to do with the way people look or their body shape, how do we define it? As adults, how can we help the kids in our life 'be healthy' without getting hung up on weight? And how can we avoid the trap of immediately assuming we know about a child's health in the first place, just by looking at their body? If health isn't a look, what is it exactly?

INTRODUCING 'HEALTH BEHAVIOURS'

On a freezing Friday in November 1986, a meeting took place which would shape the approach to health in countries all over the world over the next 30 or so years.

In the UK, The Human League were about to get to number one in the charts, Alex Ferguson (before he became a Sir) had just been appointed manager of Manchester United football club and David Bowie was dusting off his shoulder pads for the premiere of his iconic film *Labyrinth*. Over in Canada, meanwhile, 212 representatives from 38 countries met to discuss the exciting new 'health promotion' movement in public health.[11]

The first International Conference on Health Promotion was run by the WHO alongside the Canadian government and was later credited with causing millions to be spent on health initiatives around the world. The meeting saw the creation of a new charter, which recognised a number of things needed for good health: peace, shelter, education, food, income, a stable ecosystem, sustainable resources and – last but by no means least – social justice and equity.

This idea of health paved the way for a new focus on 'health behaviours' – things like exercising, making sure you get enough sleep, spending time with friends, eating a varied range of food, as well as the absence of things like smoking, binge drinking and mindless scrolling on social media.

Relating this to kids, we need to understand that a child's health is not just affected by what they eat and how much they move their body, but also by how much they interact with their mates, how much time they spend on a screen and how much sleep they're getting, to name just a few things. We'll talk more about ways to introduce healthy behaviours for kids through self-care practices in the toolkit at the end of this chapter (page 92), but for now it's useful to know that health behaviours are not just about what your kids choose to eat.

Despite what diet culture tells us, you can't know much about a person's health behaviours based on the way they look. And, perhaps more importantly, there's lots of evidence to show that if we feel good about our bodies as they are right now, we are more likely to make healthy choices for them.[12] Good body image is good for health.

If all this is making your head hurt then this advice from Dr Tosin Sotubo, a GP and founder of the Mind Body Doctor platform, will help: 'Health is complex and it's individual. It's different for each person. If you think about it as a puzzle, your body is made up of so many different pieces of the puzzle – your heart, your brain, your skin – but even if you put all that together, it still doesn't make up your health as an entirety because you've still got missing pieces. And that's where your lifestyle comes in, along with behaviour, mental health and social well-being. When you put all those things together, I think that's really what determines our health as individuals. So you can look at someone who has a nice clean bill of health, for example, no heart disease and no asthma, and you can think that looks like a healthy person. But if you're not taking into account their household set-up, their mental health, their social well-being – as well as what they're eating and putting into their body on a daily basis – you've only really got a small part of their health and well-being.'

This way of looking at health might not give instant 'results', but it's diet culture that tells us that 'results' are a number on a scale or a measurable end destination. Actual health is way more complex and multifaceted than that.

'There's nothing wrong with moving more and eating better, but let's also look at your life schedule,' says Tosin. 'Are you stressed all the time? Because stress can impact physically how your gut functions and how your heart and lungs function. So let's look at relaxation too. Rest and sleep are so important; it's your body's time to be able to rejuvenate. When you're on the go all the time, it takes a toll. Children are like sponges – it's important what you show them. So this is why it's really important for parents to look at their own health behaviours and attitudes to health, because kids will pick up on these things.'

Some light bulbs might be going off in your head while you're reading this, but just in case you need some further persuasion that making kids feel good about their bodies (regardless of what they look like) is good for their health, it might help to have a look at some of the evidence showing the cost on health that bad body image takes.

In 2017 researchers in the US found that adolescent girls who thought they were 'too fat' were more likely to drink alcohol and smoke, while adolescent boys who thought they were 'too skinny' were more likely to smoke, and boys who considered themselves 'too fat' were more likely to binge drink.[13] So not only does bad body image make kids less likely to do things

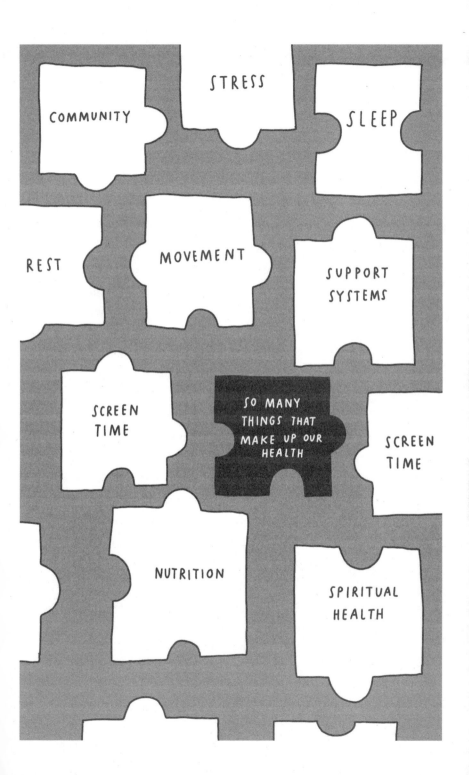

that are good for their health, it can lead to kids making choices that are actively bad for it.

WEIGHT STIGMA

Weight stigma is a form of discrimination based on a person's weight. When it comes to kids, weight stigma can also affect the parents, where assumptions are made about the parents of children in higher weight bodies. One look at Twitter or a newspaper article about 'overweight kids' and you'll see comments blaming and shaming the parents, assuming that the mums and dads of kids in bigger bodies are lazy, stupid, badly educated or just plain neglectful. These comments aren't shrouded in secrecy – there's no end of media commentators, public-facing experts and even politicians ready to put their name to these types of opinions.

Weight-based discrimination is often veiled as health concern (also known as 'concern trolling') and can happen everywhere, including in school, at home and at the doctor's. And research shows it's getting worse – in the US, weight-based discrimination went up by 66 per cent in the decade between 2002 and 2012.[14] Common stereotypes included seeing people in higher weight bodies as lazy, greedy and non-compliant. The research found that these opinions were held everywhere – from schools to employers, from doctors to the media.

One possible explanation both for the intensity of weight stigma and the fact that many people assume their bias around weight is 'helping' rather than harming, is because we're still largely unaware of all the different factors that contribute to someone's weight. We see weight (like health) as all down to personal behaviour or 'bad habits', rather than recognising there are many different factors that contribute to weight, including our genetics and the environment in which we live.[15] This oversimplification of the causes of weight gain can justify the belief for some that they're 'being cruel to be kind'.

The fact that this type of discrimination is still widely viewed as acceptable is, according to award-winning speaker, coach and educator Dana Suchow, one of the things making it so hard for parents to help their kids have a positive body image.

'Parents come to me because they think they're bad and they're failing their children because their children are plus-size,' says Dana. 'And when we start doing the work and going deeper it turns out they're afraid of being labelled bad parents, or other parents not liking them or not talking to them. They're very severely embarrassed that they're the parent with the plus-size kid. These parents get stuck, where they're bad parents for having plus-size kids, but they're also bad parents for wanting their kids to lose weight. I truly believe these parents are trying their best. They're doing what the government has told them, what doctors have told them, what society has told them. They're doing what they think is right.'

But, says Dana, the impact of effectively telling a child their body is wrong – even if it comes from a place of love – can have devastating consequences. 'Kids will do anything for love. This goes back to our animal instinct to how we've been raised through evolution. Humans take a very long time to get up out of the nest and learn and grow and talk and feed ourselves and hunt for ourselves. Babies and kids depend on adults for survival; that's how they learn to navigate the world and how they learn social skills and all these other things. Therefore, if you have a parent/teacher/guardian/doctor/caregiver effectively saying, "If you don't change how you look I'm not going to love you/

you're not going to be picked for the team/I'm not going to call on you in class/other kids are going to dislike you", that kid is going to do everything in their power to change their body. And so, unfortunately, we are starting kids on eating disorders, body image issues, trauma and PTSD, very young. We're setting kids up on yo-yo diets, cycles of self-hate, and it's all because these children want our approval.'

When we see how badly society treats people in higher weight bodies, and we are constantly told the solution to improving health is to lose weight, it seems kind of surprising that any parent *wouldn't* be tempted to put their child on a diet. But what if the health headlines are wrong? What if they're not telling us the full story?

The common idea that we're presented with is that fat = unhealthy. But as we heard from Christy Harrison in the last chapter, there's a persuasive body of evidence to show it's not the fat causing the problems but the cycle of weight loss and regain, coupled with the stigma of living in a larger body that are the problem (see page 57).

Various studies cited in a major 2007 report from researchers in the US called 'Stigma, Obesity and the Health of the Nation's Children' found that weight stigma has 'serious consequences for emotional and physical health' and the weight-based discrimination that children in larger bodies face 'could hinder their social, emotional and academic development and exacerbate adverse medical outcomes that they already face, such as impaired glucose tolerance, insulin resistance, hypertension, dyslipidemia and long-term consequences for cardiovascular and liver morbidity'.[16]

The authors of this report, Rebecca M. Puhl and Janet D. Latner, also said, 'It could be that bias experienced by obese individuals creates a vicious cycle in which exposure to and internalisation of stigma increases cortisol and metabolic abnormalities, which in turn further increases abdominal fat and perpetuates obesity, leading to additional stigma.'

Fat shaming children isn't just bad for their physical and mental health – the shame and stigma themselves could actively be contributing to their weight too.

One of the earliest and most well-known studies into weight stigma and kids took place in 1961.[17] This study was replicated in 2003 and it found that things have gotten worse.[18] In the original study, 640 school kids aged 10 to 11 in America were shown six pictures of children and asked to rank them in terms of who they'd most like to be friends with. Four of the children pictured were disabled, with one child shown as a wheelchair user, one child on crutches, one child with an amputated hand and one child with a facial disfigurement. Of the other two (nondisabled) children pictured, one was in a higher weight body and one was what researchers described as 'average weight'. The child in the higher weight body was ranked last and the least likeable every single time. When researchers did this study again in 2003 it was the same story, although this time the distance between the average rankings had increased by over 40 per cent compared with the 1961 study.

Various studies also show that weight stigma can cause an increased risk of body dissatisfaction, which can lead to a higher chance of eating disorders later on, low self-esteem (a 1997 study found that 69 per cent of kids believed if they lost weight they'd have more friends) and even, in some cases, suicidal thoughts.[19]

When weight-based discrimination is so common and so deeply damaging, and the mainstream narrative on health is so constantly focused on weight, and the idea we have total control over our weight, it's unsurprising anyone would think the solution to helping a child would be to change the child's body. But if we really care about health, perhaps we need to redirect some of our energy, time and money away from 'fixing' kids' bodies and into fixing society instead.

MENTAL HEALTH IS HEALTH

Can you remember the last time you had a really bad day? How did you feel? Were you upset? Angry? Frustrated? Now how did that show up in your body? The same is true for kids.

Our emotions often appear in really physical ways – a racing heart, a knot of anxiety in the pit of our stomach, nausea. In fact, researchers now know that when we feel emotional pain through being socially excluded the same areas of the brain get activated as when we feel physical pain.[20] This is because our mental health and our physical health are not two separate things: they are one and the same.

In the past few years conversations around mental health have become less taboo, but as adults we need to be aware of the ways in which our children's physical health is impacted by their mental health – and vice versa. And we need to remember that body image issues are a mental health issue.

Natasha Devon MBE is a campaigner, author and researcher on mental health and related issues, including body image and gender. 'The mind and the body don't exist in silos,' explains Natasha. 'They impact one another. For example, eight in ten primary school-aged children who go to their school nurse complaining of stomach ache are suffering with anxiety. Long-term physical illness and chronic pain has also (unsurprisingly) been linked to depression. So really when discussing or assessing health we need to take into account the whole person. In some distant future, I believe we'll stop using the terms "mental health" and "physical health" and just call it all "health".'

A few years ago, if you'd asked me to tell you five words I associated with the word 'fitness' I'd probably have come up words like 'Lycra', 'gym' and 'hardcore scary workout', and if you follow #fitspo-style accounts on Instagram then this might be what you would come up with too. But mental fitness is, explains Natasha, just as important a fitness as the type you try to hone at the gym.

'Mental fitness refers to the skills the individual has developed to nurture their mental health and combat symptoms of any mental health issue, as well as the support they have available to them. A person with maximum "resilience" has lots of people to talk to, lots of activities which support their mental well-being and a good level of emotional literacy.'

Mainstream conversations around health tend to focus on the importance of improving children's physical fitness and stamina, but there are many things we can do to help children stay mentally fit too, says Natasha. 'A really simple first step is to give children the means to "empty their stress bucket". This means carving out time every day to do an endorphin-creating activity to counteract the impact of inevitable everyday stress and anxiety. The best ways to create endorphins are physical activity and creativity (music, art, drama and dance). Of course, these also happen to be the subjects which have been systematically devalued and defunded within the education system over the past decade, which goes at least some way to explaining the rise in mental ill health in young people during that time.' (Remember this bit because we're going to come back to the impact of austerity on health in a minute.)

So what's the point in prioritising mental fitness? And why is it so important? As Natasha explains, it could be the difference between life and death in some cases:

'Having an awareness of mental health in all conversations with children and young people helps them to develop emotional literacy and awareness, which will in turn give them a means of communicating if they experience mental health issues (being heard and understood is a key psychological human need), as well as the means to support peers who go through challenges with their mental health. It will also give children the ability to catch any mental health problems early, which is absolutely crucial – the evidence shows the earlier an issue is identified the easier it is to treat and/or manage. When we just focus on physical health, children learn that a problem isn't important unless you can see it. The worst-case scenario is that this might increase their risk of suicide, as they constantly dismiss invisible psychological distress as "not worthy" of attention.'

The toolkit at the end of this chapter (page 92) includes some ideas for ways to empty your kids' stress bucket, and increase their mental fitness, as well as helping them connect with their bodies. These will have a direct impact on both their health and their body image. But first, let's talk about health and society, because this is important.

INEQUALITY IS BAD FOR HEALTH

When health is simplified as just being about what we eat and how much we move our bodies, and parents are told that to improve their children's health they need to focus all their efforts on managing their diet, this not only ignores all the other things that make up a child's overall health, but it also conveniently ignores the role society plays in their health.

Remember that concept of 'healthism' we talked about on page 70 and how this notion that health is all down to individual responsibility conveniently lets policymakers off the hook? Let's get into that for a minute.

Did you know that in England, people living in the most deprived areas of the country are statistically likely to experience health problems twenty years earlier in their lives than those in more affluent areas?[21] And as far as life expectancy is concerned, men in the most deprived areas live an average of nine years less than those in the least deprived areas, while this figure is seven years for women.

In 2010 a landmark report on health inequalities in the UK was published.[22] Nicknamed 'The Marmot Review' (after the review's chair, Michael Marmot), the 'Fair Society, Healthy Lives' report outlined six things that needed to happen to reduce health inequalities in the UK, which included 'giving every child the best start in life'.

Here's the opening paragraph of the report:

'People with higher socioeconomic position in society have a greater array of life chances and more opportunities to lead a flourishing life. They also have better health. The two are linked: the more favoured people are, socially and economically, the better their health. This link between social conditions and health is not a footnote to the "real" concerns with health – health care and unhealthy behaviours – it should become the main focus.'

Ten years on, the results are in, and they make pretty devastating reading. The 2020 updated report found that people can now expect to spend *more* of their lives in poor health compared with ten years ago, and that improvements to life expectancy have stalled – and even got worse for the poorest 10 per cent of women in the UK.[23] The report found that the health gap has grown between wealthy and deprived areas, and that if you live in a deprived area of the North East you can expect to live nearly five years less than someone living in a similarly deprived area in London.

If we really care about improving the health of the nation's children, we need to care about reducing inequality, because inequality is bad for health. I'm not suggesting that as you are reading this, right now, you have the power to single-handedly eradicate socioeconomic inequalities in the UK (unless you're the prime minister possibly), but it's important to keep in mind, because so often the 'But what about health?' question ignores the impact of inequality on children's health.

ANOTHER WAY: INTRODUCING HEALTH AT EVERY SIZE

If that last section made for bleak reading, this one will leave you feeling hopeful. We're going to hear about a different approach to health that is more inclusive, kind and, importantly, more effective if you want to improve the health of your kids (and yourself).

'Health at Every Size' (or HAES) is a weight-neutral approach to health, which has its history in the sixties, when activists started raising awareness about the negative impact on the increasingly promoted idea that thin bodies were better bodies. We're going to hear more about this movement in the next chapter, but it's useful to know that there would likely be no current-day dialogue about HAES, body acceptance and intuitive eating, without the work of those original activists.

In their book *Health at Every Size*, Lindo (formerly Linda) Bacon, PhD, explains that the HAES approach 'supports people of all sizes in addressing health directly by adopting healthy behaviours'.[24] If you've ever stressed about how healthy your kids are or worried that you've put on a few pounds at Christmas and so you must automatically be 'unhealthy', then this approach to health will be eye-opening for you. It's inclusive, it takes into consideration all the stuff we've talked about so far in this chapter, and – importantly – it's evidence-based.

As with any study into anything, it's important to know where the money funding the research is coming from. The research programme cited in Lindo Bacon's book was publicly funded as they felt there was a conflict of interest with accepting research money from private interest. This is something to bear in mind with any research, but particularly with studies which show the benefits of diets. Often, the money for the study will be stumped up by a company with a stake in the outcome. This means there's a vested interest in showing a particular set of results – and, as we've already seen, the diet industry is a multi-billion-dollar industry, and any researchers who have found evidence that doesn't perpetuate the thin = better narrative that the industry relies upon have often faced intense criticism from their peers.

Randomised controlled clinical trials showed that the HAES approach helped to improve blood pressure and health behaviours, as well as self-esteem and body image.[25] There's also evidence to show that the HAES approach achieves these health outcomes more successfully than weight-loss treatments and without any of the negative side effects associated with diets. In Lindo Bacon's research cited in the book, a group of women were put into two control groups: one which followed a traditional weight-loss programme and one which followed the HAES programme. The health outcomes of the HAES group were better in all cases, but what's also interesting is that the self-esteem of the dieting group plummeted, while the HAES group became more empowered. In Lindo Bacon's words: 'Happier, healthier people feel more empowered and make better choices.'

Before we get into the basic components of the HAES approach, let's quickly go back to the elephant in the room: the weight thing. As we've already seen, weight is complex and much of what we think we know about weight is flawed. But we haven't yet discussed 'set point theory', which is a way of recognising genetic diversity that goes against the diet culture perspective steeped in weight bias, telling us that our weight (and our children's weight) is all down to personal control.

Set point theory is based on the evidence that our bodies have an internal weight regulation system, a bit like an inbuilt thermostat for weight. It's a biological force that we are born with and the further we fiddle with it the harder our bodies will work to bring it back to its natural set point. There is no one-size-fits-all set point, and biological diversity means one person's natural 'healthy' weight – or set point – won't be the same as another's.

There are lots of things that influence a body's set point, including the genes you inherit from your parents, the stress you're under and the environment you live in. But rather than trying to alter the body's inbuilt weight thermostat, the HAES paradigm focuses on giving you a framework to live your life in a healthy way *without* weight being the focus.

This approach recognises that our bodies are not all meant to be the same, and that there are limits to the control we have over our weight through healthy means. When we apply this to children, whose bodies are growing and changing all the time, it becomes even more urgent to teach them the tools to trust and connect with their bodies, and recognise what things make their bodies feel good. If we encourage this natural connection, this will empower them to engage in more of those 'health-promoting behaviours' we heard about earlier, while also meaning they're less likely to do things that might risk both their physical and mental health as they pursue a 'health look'.

The HAES approach includes three important areas: respect, critical awareness and compassionate self-care. Under the respect banner is the practice of celebrating body diversity and honouring differences in size, age, race, ethnicity, gender, dis/ability, sexual orientation, religion, class and other human attributes. The critical awareness area includes the ability to challenge scientific and cultural assumptions, as well as valuing your own body's knowledge and lived experience. And compassionate self-care is (unsurprisingly) not just about bubble baths and avocado on toast, but about finding the joy in moving your body and being physically active, as well as eating in a flexible way following your body's internal cues, while 'respecting the social conditions that frame eating options'.

The ideas and toolkits throughout this book will often go back to these three areas and draw inspiration from the HAES paradigm. We'll talk about language to help children celebrate diversity, media literacy to help them decode some of the messages they're presented with and, in a minute, we're going to dive into self-care.

Giving children the tools to respect and appreciate their bodies as they are right now, as well as respecting and appreciating other bodies that are not like their own, is good for their health. A child who is connected to their body will be more likely to make choices that feel good for it, including eating and moving in a way that feels good. And a child who knows that the worth of their body cannot be measured by its outside appearance will have a solid foundation of body respect to carry them through life and continue to make these healthy choices – as well as being able to better bat away some of the negative messages that might impact their body image.

BODY HAPPY KIDS TOOLKIT
Self-Care

The science

'Self-care isn't selfish' might sound like an overused Instagram caption, but when it comes to health it's a really important thing to remember – and one we need to teach our kids too. As we've already heard, mental health is health, and stress is bad for health. And the HAES approach sees self-care as being so important to health that it cites 'compassionate self-care' as an important foundation of the framework.

'Compassionate self-care' includes moving your body and eating in a way that feels good – and we'll be covering these areas later in the book with dedicated toolkits for food and exercise for kids (see pages 142 and 162). But there's another element of self-care which is just as important for health but often overlooked. It's this element we'll be focusing on in this toolkit.

All of the activities in this toolkit will help to reduce stress, boost mental well-being, improve sleep (also a very important aspect of health) and enhance the social well-being of the kids in your care. While this toolkit isn't a menu plan of what 'healthy foods' to feed your kids (we're going to look at food in Chapter 5), it does contain activities and ideas which are just as important to the health of your kids as what they eat.

Don't just take it from me though. Meditation expert Aisha Carrington says without self-care, there can be no health: 'Self-care is the umbrella that everything else comes underneath. Rather than thinking about it as an add-on or something extra people should do, it needs to become just part of your life, because if you're not taking care of yourself this will have a huge impact on all parts of your health.'

And, according to Aisha, when it comes to kids, it's never too young to start: 'One nugget of self-care a day is as important as making sure your kids brush their teeth. If it's not prioritised, we'll see the impact of that as they get older.'

In this busy technology-fuelled age, self-care is even more important. We spend a lot of time thinking about our kids' extra-curricular activities and stressing over what clubs they're taking part in, but Aisha says we need to redirect some of that energy to prioritising quiet moments too.

'If you think about it in a religious context, there was a time when it was standard for most people to pray every day and for children to go to Sunday school. Well, praying is meditation.

It takes you outside of yourself. People prayed for other people and they prayed for themselves. They set an intention for the day and it helped them stop and take a breath. I'm not saying you need to start praying – or even meditating – but just teaching children to connect with their breath and to learn how to slow down and connect with their bodies will have a hugely positive impact on their overall health. And if they start these little forms of self-care early it will just become a natural part of their life that they won't need to relearn later on.'

The tool: the self-care for kids starter kit

Use this starter kit to help introduce your kids to ideas around self-care. Try to do one thing every day and build it into your child's daily routine in just the same way as you encourage them to brush their teeth. Remember, you wouldn't run a marathon without some kind of training, and you can't build mental fitness without some practice either. So consider this starter kit as just as important a foundation for their overall health as how many vegetables they eat every day.

Community

Social connections raise self-esteem and are a huge part of overall health. What's more, experts say strong communities are good for health (and loneliness is bad for health). With that in mind, here are some self-care ideas based on fostering community:

» Make connections with a local nursing home and take your kids to regularly visit.
» Join Girlguiding UK, the Scouts or another youth group.

» Get involved with your school PTA group – many groups will allow older children to help at events such as fairs or discos.

» Join a community grow scheme in your area with your family (see Resources, page 233) – there's also evidence to show that gardening is good for body image so this activity has a double bonus!

It doesn't even have to be an organised initiative – it could be a play date at your local park or a coffee morning at another parent's house. There are apps that enable you to meet other parents and connect with families looking to socialise with others too (see Resources, page 233).

Mindfulness

Mindfulness is a skill that allows children (and adults) to be completely involved in the present moment, both physically and emotionally. This can help to reduce stress and boost happiness. Experts say the best way to teach kids to be mindful is to be mindful yourself, so perhaps you could try some of the following activities together:

Meditation: You don't need to sit down and close your eyes for ten minutes (although that does sound lovely). There are many resources to help teach children early meditation skills (see Resources, page 233). But even just encouraging children to stop for a minute or so and take a few deep breaths, and to really focus on one single thing right now, is a positive health habit.

Colouring: As we learned in the toolkit from Chapter 1 (page 36), colouring is a great mindfulness activity. You could use the art therapy affirmation idea from that toolkit for some regular colouring inspiration.

Jigsaws: Jigsaw puzzles are another great mindfulness activity for children as they encourage them to stay in the present. If you can, get involved too!

Journaling: Keeping a journal to write down thoughts and feelings is a brilliant way to not only process emotions but to let go of worries too. Older children might like to use their journal as part of a 'worry window', giving their brain permission to come back to the worry later on without focusing on it all day.

Get outside: A simple walk can be turned into a mindfulness activity. Encourage your child to focus on the sounds around them and the things they can see. If you're feeling particularly creative you could stop along the way and make a daisy chain – a totally free mindfulness activity!

Senses

A key aspect of mindfulness is to tune in to your senses. Interestingly, this will also help children connect with their bodies, which, as we know, is essential for positive body image. These self-care activities are based on using the senses to slow down, focus and reconnect:

Find their happy smell: Whether it's cut grass or a particular essential oil, or even the smell of sun cream, we all have a smell that we associate with happiness. Encourage your child to think about what their 'happy smell' is, and then use that smell to ground them in the moment. It might be putting some sun

· worry window ·

cream on, or dabbing some essential oil on a handkerchief, or even going for a walk in a pine forest or by the sea if you're able to – any way to get your child connected to the smells that make them happy is a good thing.

Make a glitter jar: A glitter jar is a great tool to help children meditate if they struggle to sit still. Fill a jar with hot water, glue, food colouring and eco-friendly glitter. You can use this jar to explain to a child that their mind is like the jar, full of swirling thoughts. When you shake the jar the thoughts go everywhere. But as it stays still the glitter settles. Watching it settle can help to calm down the mind.

Create a chill-out den: Sometimes the novelty of having a cosy, private space is a great way to encourage children to snuggle down and relax when they'd usually be on the go. Fill your den with cushions and a range of textures to get them to use the sense of touch to ground themselves in the moment. Your den could even be outside on a sunny day.

Have a kitchen disco: We'll talk more about the benefits of movement as self-care in Chapter 6 (you can use the movement planner tool from that chapter as part of your kids' self-care toolkit too – see page 164), but I wanted to include kitchen discos here because they're such an easy, mood-boosting and, most importantly, *fun* form of self-care. This activity incorporates both movement and sound to get the endorphins going, boost mood and reconnect with the body.

Create a piece of self-care art: Can your kids draw a picture of themselves in the middle of a piece of paper then add lots of self-care activities around the edge? Or maybe they can draw a circle with all their ideas as a 'self-care wheel'. Older children and teenagers might like to use those graphic design tools we talked about in the first toolkit on page 37 to create a self-care starter kit that's completely personal to them.

CHAPTER 4

Don't Ban the F Word: Talking to Kids About Bodies

There is huge power in language, and children pick up on this quickly. But what if our attempts to shield kids from some of the words that have been so hurtful to us in the past may be having the opposite effect? What if banning some words and giving too much attention to others is actually damaging the relationship our children have with their bodies, now and in the future?

In this chapter we are going to explore how we can have better conversations with our kids about how they feel about their bodies and how we can reframe how we think about certain words so they are no longer steeped in negativity. We'll be hearing from some brilliant activists and educators on this too.

You'll also find a toolkit at the end (page 117), which will help you navigate these conversations with your children and give them a wider vocabulary to talk about how they're feeling, because sometimes when children (and adults) express negative feelings about their bodies, there's another emotion hiding underneath. Our bodies often get the blame for other uncomfortable feelings, but as we're going to find out, fat is not a feeling.

THE POWER OF WORDS

Do you remember that childhood rhyme, 'Sticks and stones may break my bones, but words can never hurt me'? I never thought it made sense because words *can* hurt. They carry a huge amount of power. Entire societies and systems of oppression are built on the weight of words. The saying should be: 'Sticks and stones may break my bones, but words can pierce my soul to its very core and break my heart into a thousand tiny pieces before trampling on the empty shell of my being.' Or something like that.

As a child, I learned quickly that one of the worst things you could call someone in the playground was 'fat'. It wasn't enough to call someone 'stupid' or 'ugly'. If you wanted to really twist the knife you'd add the word 'fat' to round off the insult properly. In films, on TV and in books, fat became a signifier for a character's personality traits. The message couldn't have been any clearer if it was written across the sky: fat = bad. I grew up believing fat was so bad that not only did I fear becoming fat but I also grew up believing that in order to be kind I had to do the opposite of what mean people did. And this meant rushing to reassure people, 'You're not fat!', which confirmed that, yes, being fat was the very worst thing someone could be.

I wasn't alone. As a parent years later, I heard how the negative connotations that came with the word 'fat' persisted. At

toddler groups I overheard parents telling kids not to say 'the F word' as if 'fat' was worse than any swear word their tot might utter. And while this came from a well-intentioned place, it continued to perpetuate the idea that fat = bad.

Along with 'fat', the insults that were hurled around the playground were based on gender or ability or sexuality. Any body type that didn't fit the mainstream version of beauty (thin, white, cisgendered, nondisabled and heterosexual) was seen as less than, and often formed the basis of an insult.

I clearly remember walking down the corridor on my first day at secondary school, with a new short hairstyle and a ruck-sack strapped to my back that was almost as tall as me, only to be crushed by a group of Year 10 boys openly laughing at me. 'Oh, look! It's a little man!' they chanted. My undeveloped breasts and short hairstyle saw me live with the nickname 'Little Man' right through Year 7. For those boys, the best way they could assert their own power and take away mine was to criti-cise my appearance and suggest I was somehow 'other' because (even though I was thin, white and cisgendered) my short hair-style and non-curvy frame didn't live up to the beauty ideal they rated girls by.

Twenty-five years later and things have changed, but also not so much. The language we use around bodies is the founda-tion propping up views which continue to marginalise children who don't fit into what society tells them they should look like. And even if children do look the way society tells them they should, they are taught early on to police their bodies and to conform in order to be accepted by other kids and avoid being bullied in the school corridors.

There is hope though. Because if we challenge some of the normalised attitudes that continue to exist through the words we do and don't use, and actually have these conversations with our kids, we give our children the power to be free in their bodies and to accept the bodies of others. This is what this chapter is all about.

Celebrating size diversity is good for body image

1967 was the year of debut albums from The Doors, Jimi Hendrix, The Velvet Underground, David Bowie and Pink Floyd. It was also the year of the first 'Fat In', a gathering of 500 people in New York's Central Park protesting over the discrimination of people in bigger bodies. Carrying signs painted with slogans like 'Fat Power' and 'Think Fat', the group ate snacks and burned diet books and photos of the supermodel of the day, Twiggy.[1]

A few months later an article appeared in American newspaper *The Saturday Evening Post* titled 'More people should be FAT'.[2] Written by Llewellyn Louderback, the article was a response to the discrimination that his wife faced for living in a larger body and was one of the first defences of fatness in the mainstream press. Louderback later met up with a guy called Bill Fabrey and the National Association to Aid Fat Americans (NAAFA), formed in 1969. This is now the National Association to Advance Fat Acceptance, which holds periodic conventions with workshops and runs advocacy initiatives including the Equality at Every Size Program, 'providing education and support for changing the anti-discrimination laws throughout the US to include rights for fat people'.[3]

NAAFA was not the only group calling for civil rights for people in bigger bodies and reclaiming the word fat. The Fat

Underground was an LA activist group run by women in the seventies. It believed mainstream feminism failed to include women of size and called for a radical change to society with their Fat Liberation Manifesto, demanding human respect and recognition for fat people. They saw diet culture as a tool for patriarchal oppression, a way for society to exert control over women's bodies.

Fast forward 60 years and where have we got to? The word 'fat' is still seen as a negative word in the mainstream and there is still a basic denial of respect and recognition for people in bigger bodies, including children. The rhetoric around the 'war on obesity' means adults are so concerned about the kids in their life either being fat or becoming fat, they're unwittingly creating environments that make it almost impossible for kids to love their bodies or engage in health-promoting behaviours that might make their bodies feel good.

Nicola Salmon is a fat-positive fertility coach and author of the book *Fat and Fertile: How to Get Pregnant in a Bigger Body*. 'Growing up I was an average-sized child, but maybe bigger than my peers, and the word "fat" was bandied around for me and it was so shameful,' says Nicola. 'In my teens and twenties I was fat, and my whole existence was based around trying to make my body smaller – that took so much physical and mental energy, and time and money. It was only when I had my son, who is now six, that I decided to give up dieting and weighing myself because I knew I could not pass it on to him.'

Nicola explains that, for her, using the word 'fat' as a descriptor for her body came when she started to find other people in the fat acceptance movement. 'I realised it was OK to be fat and I didn't need to be a before picture, and I wasn't a thin person trying to get out of a fat costume – it was such a revelation to me. It took me a long time to become comfortable with the word "fat" because for so many years of my life I'd associated being thin with being happy. And I really had to get my head around the fact I could be fat and happy.'

When it comes to reclaiming some of the words that have been weaponised against people in bigger bodies, it's complicated. Because while 'fat' should simply be just a descriptive word, it still comes loaded with fear and negativity for many, and any person with thin privilege – including children – needs to be mindful of this. So how can we introduce these ideas with nuance and sensitivity to young children who simply won't understand the context, and remove the shame and moral judgement from 'fat' without inadvertently giving kids the green light to go out and unintentionally hurt someone's feelings?

'I tell my boys that we don't comment on other people's bodies,' says Nicola. 'I encourage them to call my body fat – I want them to not find that word repulsive or difficult to say. But I don't want them to then go and do harm in the playground and use that word non-offensively but for people to take offence to it. So we don't comment on other people's bodies without permission. This is an important lesson in consent too.'

In an effort not to offend, many people will use terms like 'overweight' and 'obesity', which seem fine given that these are the words often used by doctors and health professionals, right? Well, no, actually. Because, again, it's perpetuating the idea that one type of body is better than another. Being 'over' or 'under' weight still assumes there is a 'perfect' weight, and it still makes weight the measure of health.

'For me, when I am labelled as "obese" I'm labelled as a problem, as an outlier, as someone who has these inherent risks and problems with their health,' explains Nicola. 'And I know that's not true. I don't have a disease that's obesity, I am just in a fat body, and those two things aren't the same thing. So for me, obesity is this falsehood and a way of describing fat bodies as a problem and something that needs to be fixed when we know that body diversity has been around as long as humans have.'

There is so much negativity around the word 'fat' that often adults and children alike will use it to describe another feeling. Perhaps they are feeling tired, anxious, unmotivated or over-whelmed – it often gets lumped under the word 'fat'. At the end of this chapter you'll find a toolkit to help with this (page 117). By expanding our children's vocabulary to help them identify the emotion they're actually experiencing, they will be less quick to label the feeling as 'fat', because fat is not a feeling.

Celebrating ability diversity is good for body image

When it comes to descriptions of health and the language used to denote what is 'healthy' or 'unhealthy' it's not just fatphobia we need to watch out for – it's ableism too.

Ableism is discrimination in favour of nondisabled people and is 100 per cent not compatible with creating a body happy environment for children to thrive in. If we're trying to teach our kids that all bodies are good bodies, and everyone has the right to feel good in their body regardless of how it looks or functions, we need to get comfortable with the language around disability and start having these conversations with our children. Disability activist Nina Tame explains why: 'I can only speak for me and the community I know, but for so long "disabled" was seen as this horrible word. Many would use the word "differently abled" instead. But this feels patronising and othering – if you're not "disabled" but are "differently abled", who is disabled? I talk a lot about the word "disabled" being a neutral word, because so many people see it as negative, as something that should be pitied or something that is "so inspiring". Automatically all this stuff is put on a word that can mean a billion different things depending on who's existing inside that word.'

Reclaiming the word 'disabled' and using it in a neutral way around kids is so important, says Nina, who advocates for parents to have these chats from day one. 'There's often a tendency to think "everybody's the same" and so not to bring up differences, but we're not the same. As kids get older, they realise this and just make up their own minds. So I think it's really important to have representation in your children's lives through toys and books and the TV shows you watch, and then to have conversations about it. Say "That person is disabled" or "That person is a wheelchair user." Talk about it and have the language to just say those words in a very neutral way. It doesn't have to be a complicated thing. It can simply be: "Some people are disabled and that might mean they walk differently to you, or they think differently to you, or they can't see or hear, or they might use a wheelchair."'

It's also useful to point out the difference between talking about 'someone with a disability' and 'a disabled person', because they are not the same thing. 'The medical model sees a disabled person as having a disability and the disability is what disables them,' says Nina. 'Whereas the social model sees a disabled person as having an impairment and what disables them is society's weird attitudes or lack of access. This puts the responsibility on everyone because the world is inaccessible, and it doesn't have to be.'

Remember how we need to fix society and not our bodies? This is another reminder of that. Arming children with the language to talk about *all* bodies, and not to value one type of body over another could help them to avoid a lifetime of not feeling good enough in their bodies, as well as giving them the tools to be allies for and to advocate for the rights of those whose bodies may function differently to their own.

Celebrating gender diversity is good for body image

How do the words we use around gender and sexuality inform the way children feel about their bodies? This might feel like a massive leap, but stick with me, because these are subjects that can impact our children's body image from the moment they are born, whether they conform to the gender they were assigned at birth or not, and however they later define their sexuality.

I first noticed the ingrained ideas we have in our society around gender when I was pregnant with my first daughter and was bombarded with the 'Is it a boy or a girl?' question. Gender reveal parties were big news, and it soon became apparent you were either 'team pink' (girl) or 'team blue' (boy).

Along with the colours pink and blue came a predefined set of ideas that were put on the baby before they'd even taken their first breath. Carrying a boy? Kit him out in dinosaur onesies, give him toy cars and teach him to be strong. Oh, it's a girl? Here are some pink ribbons and a doll – and don't forget to tell her she's pretty! This is called 'gender stereotyping' and these stereotypes are bad for body image.

In 2019 The Fawcett Society published research show-ing the lifelong impact of gender stereotyping in childhood.[4] The research found that 45 per cent of people have experi-enced gender stereotyping in childhood and were expected to behave a certain way due to their gender, and more than half of people said this had constrained their career choices. A further 44 per cent said gender stereotyping had harmed their personal relationships. The research also found that by two years old children are aware of gender and, as early as six years old, chil-dren associate intelligence with being male and 'niceness' with being female.

So what does all this have to do with body image? Gender stereotypes traditionally teach girls that it is their job to be pretty. This is reinforced by the clothes parents are encour-aged to buy (often prioritising appearance over practicality and comfort), by the fairy tales that portray princesses as 'beauti-ful' and by the way we teach girls that their appearance is an important commodity. Girls are taught to focus on how they look above all else, and to view their bodies through the lens of others so they can't fully live in and appreciate the moment.

By contrast, boys are taught to be 'strong' and 'brave', that the ideal characteristics of a man are bulging biceps and the ability not to cry. Their icons are heroic princes who do the rescuing or brave superheroes who save the world and beat up the bad guys. Any boy who doesn't live up to what he believes a boy 'should' be risks feeling insecure in his body. And then, because of the way boys are often told to contain their emotions ('man up' being one example), he may be less likely to articulate those emotions for fear of being labelled 'girly'. This could be one explanation for why body image issues have historically been seen as a 'girls' problem' – it's not that boys don't suffer with this stuff, it's that they fear the judgement that will come with sharing their insecurities.

We'll talk more about this in Chapters 8 and 10, but for now it's important to know that opting for neutral language that doesn't reinforce gender stereotypes and gives children the chance to explore their identity can be a powerful tool in creating body happy environments for kids. This stuff is hard to erase straight away, but just thinking twice about the types of words you use to describe your children or how you compliment them can have an impact. For example, do you regularly refer to your daughter as 'pretty' and 'nice' but your son as 'strong' or 'brave'?

Taking the stereotypes out of what it means to be a boy or girl may also create an environment that allows gender non-conforming children and, later on, older kids who identify as LGBTQ+ to be themselves without fear of judgement or shame.[5] This means recognising and respecting people's pronouns, as well as providing a safe and accepting environment for kids to know they are loved and accepted unconditionally just as they are. For teachers this could be something as simple as saying 'hello students' at the beginning of a class instead of 'hello boys and girls', and for parents it could be providing books with a diverse range of characters and then having conversations about these characters. This is hugely important if we want *all* children to feel at peace in their bodies. Again, it's getting away from those narrow beauty ideals that tell children one type of body (and one type of person) is more worthy and valued than another.

Zoey and Kelly Allen are LGBTQ+ content creators who run the platform Our Transitional Life. They were married

DON'T BAN THE F WORD

before Zoey came out as transgender and they started their blog supporting Zoey through her transition. 'Before Zoey came out as trans, our daughter already disliked words like "fireman", "policeman" and "human" and wanted to know why we couldn't all just be called "people",' says Kelly. 'We started to look at gender identity as a whole and our daughter just got it. I'd say her knowledge about gender identity is probably further along than mine because I have to retrain my brain due to the generation I grew up in. But our kids haven't had to retrain anything – they've entered a world full of diversity and acceptance, and that's really beautiful.'

'Growing up, I didn't have any awareness about this,' says Zoey. 'I didn't even know the term "gay" until I was a teenager, and I definitely didn't know anything about transgender or different genders until I was in my mid-twenties because it just wasn't the world I was living in.'

This lack of awareness and narrow vocabulary around gender and identity can cause real pain, which is something Zoey explains she's experienced first-hand: 'I've stored up so much through my life and that's not been healthy for me. It's important to teach children that regardless of your gender it's OK to cry. Kelly and I talk to our children a lot about the importance of being open and honest with their feelings and if they are angry or stressed we encourage them to talk about it or draw it or vent it in a healthy way.'

If you don't know where to start with this, then the toolkit at the end of this chapter will help (page 117). It's a starting point to help children learn to identify their emotions, which will help them develop emotional literacy and the ability to have conversations about why they might be feeling a certain way. This all comes back to body image because not only will developing a wider emotional vocabulary help children process their feelings (regardless of their gender) but it might help them to avoid blaming an uncomfortable emotion on their bodies in the first place. More on that later.

WHEN IT'S TIME TO STOP TALKING ABOUT BODIES ALTOGETHER

So far, we've talked about celebrating different types of bodies and the importance of teaching children that no one type of body is better than another. And this *is* important. But I also think it's important to teach children that they are so much *more* than their bodies; if we get in the trap of continuously talking about bodies – even in a positive way – we risk inadvertently giving kids the opposite message. Using neutral language (and sometimes saying nothing at all) can help us avoid this trap.

In 2018 a group of researchers did a study into the impact of 'fat talk' on children (note: the fact that negative body talk is even termed 'fat talk' shows how far we still need to go in terms of neutralising the word 'fat').[6] They found that the more children were exposed to negative talk about bodies, the less likely they were to eat mindfully or appreciate their bodies in terms of how they function. On the flip side of this, experts also say that constantly focusing on how much you love the way your body looks can cause problems because it can reinforce the idea for children that their appearance is the most important thing they have to offer the world.

Dr Lindsay Kite is co-director of the US-based non-profit Beauty Redefined, which she runs with her sister, Dr Lexie Kite. They have also authored the book *More Than a Body*. The organisation works to help people – particularly women and girls – build body image resilience to overcome the negative impact of objectification.

'The ways we talk about bodies – our own, others', even strangers' or celebrities' – plays a huge role in how children learn to understand and relate to their own bodies,' explains Lindsay. 'If we are fixating on appearance, whether positively or negatively, that teaches children that the way our bodies look is the most important thing about them. Kids will naturally wonder about bodies and how they differ from each other. When a kid you love is bullied because of their looks, it is easy to react with an immediate, "You're not ugly – you're beautiful!" But assuring someone that they are beautiful will not protect them from the pain of being called ugly. If you give looks-based comments the power to build people up, you reinforce their power to tear people down. Continuing to focus on someone's looks – even in positive ways – uses the same framework that makes appearance-based insults so hurtful. The truth is when we stop giving beauty the power to make us, we take away its power to break us.'

Instead of rushing to counteract a looks-based criticism with a looks-based compliment, Lindsay recommends encouraging children to believe they are more than a body. 'To help a girl's self-worth and help her build body image resilience, teach her she is more than beautiful. Don't reassure her that her body *looks* great. Teach her that her body *is* great. Tell her who she really is – kind, strong, talented, hilarious, intelligent, compassionate, etc. Compliment her in ways that remind her she is more than a body.'

While girls are often objectified and taught that it's their job to be pretty, boys can be told it's their job to be strong. So for boys it can be a case of teaching them that strength doesn't just look one way and that there is huge strength in kindness and vulnerability. Ultimately, no matter the gender of your child, teaching them that their body is for *doing* and not for *being looked at* is great for body image.

The same goes for the way we talk about other peoples' bodies. No matter how great you think that celebrity looks in that magazine, you don't need to comment on it. A classic example is the press attention the singer Adele got in 2020 after posting photos of herself online showing dramatic weight loss. The praise over Adele's new figure might seem harmless – or even positive – but what message does this give children? Adele is an Grammy Award-winning singer who's sold millions of albums, but judging by the focus on her body, it's the weight loss that many people saw as her biggest achievement, not her musical genius. We never know the back story to someone's weight loss and commenting on it risks perpetuating the notion that the most important thing about a person is their body.

I get it; complimenting someone's appearance is often second nature. It took me a while to fall out of the habit of doing this with my own daughters, but now instead of saying, 'Wow, you look so cool in that outfit!' I'll say something like, 'You are so creative – I love how you've picked out these colours to go together.' (This type of compliment works with kids of all genders!) I also often tell my daughters how brave, clever, kind, strong and funny they are – and they both know the mantra 'It's not my job to be pretty' by heart! If you're a parent of boys, you could switch this to 'It's not my job to be strong' instead. And if you find yourself regularly giving looks-based compliments to your kids (or anyone), now's the time to think of some other ways you can compliment them without focusing on their appearance.

BODY HAPPY KIDS TOOLKIT

How to Widen Your Child's Emotional Vocabulary

The science

Having the words to talk about bodies and discuss our emotions is good for body image. But in a culture where talking about feelings doesn't come naturally and words have been used to create shame around bodies, this is easier said than done. This is where this toolkit comes in. It's based on what we've just learned about reclaiming certain words, along with a tool designed by psychologists to give us a wider vocabulary to help name emotions. This is because naming an emotion reduces its impact. That's right – in yet another example of why our minds are amazing – scientists discovered that putting problems into words can ease emotional distress.[7]

What's this got to do with body image though? Well, not only will naming an emotion give children the ability to process that emotion but it will also mean they are less likely to wrongly identify a feeling. For example, often 'I feel fat' is the go-to descriptor when the person is actually feeling tired or lacking in energy, but because the word 'fat' is so loaded with negative meaning it's used as a label for an unhappy feeling instead. And because our brains are hardwired to feel better when we name an emotion, if we name it wrongly, we won't feel better. This means you might decide the way to feel better is to change your body, when actually the first step is to correctly name the emotion.

Anna Mathur is a psychotherapist and the author of *Mind Over Mother: Every Mum's Guide to Worry and Anxiety in the First Years*. 'We are so conditioned to diminish feelings, tuck them away, use comparison to tell ourselves we "shouldn't" be feeling a certain way,' says Anna. 'Every time we minimise or ignore an emotion, it doesn't go anywhere. But by finding the words to explain a feeling, it enables us to speak them out and process them. When speaking with clients who struggle to find the language to explain a feeling, I encourage them to think about "trying feelings on" like clothes. Name a few feelings: angry, resentful, lonely, tired, sad, fed up ... and see if one of them "fits". When we name feelings, we may feel a sudden emotional lurch towards one that resonates.'

But what if we can't recognise the emotion because we don't have the language to identify it? The Feelings Wheel was designed by Dr Gloria Willcox in the eighties to help give people a wider vocabulary to express their emotions.[8] This toolkit is based on the Feelings Wheel as a resource to give children an opportunity to describe how they are feeling.

The tool: a body happy dictionary

You can use this tool as a guide to help you explore the way you discuss bodies and feelings at home. First, here is a mini recap of what we've learned in this chapter:

> » *Fat is a descriptor:* The word 'fat' is a neutral, descriptive word, in just the same way as 'thin', 'tall' or 'short'.
> » *Your body, your description:* How you choose to describe your body is up to you. For this reason, we don't comment on other people's bodies without their consent.
> » *Differences are not bad:* Our bodies are not all meant to look or function in the same way. Talk about these differences at home with your children in a neutral way.
> » *Avoid gender stereotypes:* Gender-neutral language is good for body image. Non-appearance-based compliments are also great!

We've got the words to start talking about bodies. But now we need to find the words to talk about feelings, because our emotions are intrinsically tied up with our body image. Telling a child 'fat' is a neutral word and then not giving them the tools to explore the reasons why they say 'I feel fat' is equivalent to putting a plaster on a broken arm and hoping it will heal all by itself.

Step 1: Collect the feelings

Draw a circle and draw a horizontal line through the middle of the circle, then separate each half of the circle into three pieces. Label each section with one of the six 'core feelings': the top three with 'angry', 'scared' and 'sad', and the bottom three with 'happy', 'excited' and 'peaceful'. You might like to get your kids involved in this activity and encourage them to colour in a section with a colour they think best fits that emotion.

Now, in each part of the circle add some more words that are linked to the six core feelings:

» For 'angry': jealous, hurt, irritated, frustrated.

» For 'scared': confused, rejected, embarrassed, worried.

» For 'sad': guilty, ashamed, lonely, tired.

» For 'happy': creative, playful, hopeful, confident.

» For 'excited': amazed, energetic, restless, impatient.

» For 'peaceful': grateful, loving, accepted, content.

Step 2: Find the feeling

Now encourage your child to use the circle to identify how they are feeling right now. You can use the six 'core feelings' as a starting point (this might be where you stop for younger children) and then move on to the other words. For teenagers, you might like to look up 'Feelings Wheel' online to get an even wider range of emotions to choose from.

Step 3: Talk about the feeling

Once you've identified the feeling, talk about some of the ways it shows up in your child's body. For example, when your child is feeling angry, does their face get hot, do their shoulders tense up, do they feel like they want to shout? Explain that these are all completely normal, natural emotions and are the body's way of helping them to process that feeling – and talk about how clever their body is for talking to them in this way (this is a chance to bring some body appreciation into the conversation!).

Step 4: Draw the feeling

If you want to take the exercise further, or simply use this activity as a stand-alone one, you could ask your child to draw their feeling for you. What colours would they use? What shapes would they use? This is another way to encourage your child to talk about their feelings, and it's a mindfulness exercise too. Older children might like to create a story using some of the words they've pinpointed in the circle.

This doesn't need to be a big elaborate activity that takes up hours of your day. Once you've got the circle you can just stick it to your fridge and use it as a reference point to encourage your child to check in with their feelings every now and again.

CHAPTER 5

Let Them Eat Cake: How to Raise Happy Eaters

Food can be joy; it can be celebration, nourishment, happy memories, comfort, fuel. But it can also be scary and stressful and a source of extreme tension. This chapter covers the subject of food and kids, and how to raise children who have a happy and healthy relationship with food.

Babies are born intuitively knowing what, how much and when they want to eat, but somewhere along the way they lose that intuition. This might be through adults enforcing arbitrary rules around food (often from a place of good intention – I know, I've done it myself), external pressure from society telling them what and how much they should eat in order to look a certain way, or ideas around what is or isn't healthy. Either way, they lose it.

We're going to learn in this chapter how to raise kids who do not lose this intuition and how, as adults, we can avoid doing some of the things that might make the children in our care grow up to have a difficult relationship with food. If you've got an older child, it's not too late – much of the advice here will be useful for you too. I am not a dietician or a nutritionist, so I've sought advice from people who work in this field to share some of their expertise with you. And I've drawn on a variety of studies and research to show you that what we thought we knew about kids and food might not be the full story.

Despite the title of this chapter, it's not just about feeding kids cake 24/7. An anti-diet mentality is not anti feeding kids nutritious meals with vegetables. I feel I should make this clear right from the start, because so often the assumption is that people who are anti diets are pro feeding children nothing but doughnuts, and this simply isn't the case (although don't get me wrong; I do love a doughnut!).

What this is about is allowing children to follow their inbuilt hunger and fullness cues and have a joyful, happy and healthy relationship with their bodies which allows them to eat in a way that feels good.

'EAT UP'

I was about seven years old when I was first told to 'Eat up'. I'd been invited for tea at a friend's house and her mum had asked me how many fish fingers I wanted. I'd asked for three but could only eat two. On asking to get down from the table I was told, 'No. Eat up. Clear your plate.'

This was an alien concept to me because I was being raised in a house where 'eating up' wasn't a thing. My dad had experienced his own 'Eat up' situation as a child in primary school in the fifties, where a post-war rations mentality ruled, and good citizens did not waste food.

By the age of seven I was already well versed in my dad's childhood memory. At the age of five, he was forced to sit in front of a plate of congealed spaghetti that he refused to eat. To this day he can still remember how his stomach turned at the sight of the slimy, sticky threads of pasta, swimming in lumpy tomato sauce, and how his face burned at the humiliation of being forced to sit in front of it for hours in the corner of the classroom. It wasn't until middle age that my dad began to actually enjoy eating spaghetti again.

Every time he told this story my heart hurt at the thought of someone being humiliated in this way. And when I read about Bruce Bogtrotter in Roald Dahl's *Matilda* being forced to consume an entire chocolate cake in front of the whole school I couldn't help but think of my poor dad, in his oversized school uniform, sitting in front of a plate of cold spaghetti.

So it was a shock to be told to 'Eat up'. And an even bigger shock to be scolded for having 'eyes bigger than my belly'. Up until this moment I'd been hugely privileged to only have experienced food in a positive way. I'd never been shamed for my food choices or associated negative emotions with eating. Food was joyful – we ate around the table as a family, and it was a central part of many celebrations for us.

When I became a mum myself I realised what a gift it was that my parents gave me, because this was certainly not the norm. Reading all the different (often conflicting) weaning advice was confusing, and hearing conversations from other parents discussing food as a source of stress in their family made me nervous about introducing my own baby to solids. While I was excited to see my daughter's reactions to different foods, I was already well aware of the pressure parents are put under to feed their kids the 'right' foods and the huge amount of emotional baggage that comes with eating. I was not only scared I'd get it wrong, I was scared that my daughter's eating would somehow become a judgement on my own parenting.

And this is where things get dicey. There is so much negativity around food that it's no longer a straightforward issue of feeding. Food has become a signifier of someone's parenting ability, their social status and how much they love their children. If your child happily consumes kale then you get extra brownie points, but if they'd rather feast on Fruit Shoots then, according to some newspaper columnists and politicians, you're not just a bad parent, you're lazy, stupid and clearly don't care about the health of your child. There is also a widely held assumption that we can know everything about a child's diet just from looking at their body, and this is simply not true.

We now have to prove our parenting abilities and our social status by avoiding the 'bad' food and ramping up the 'good' food. Diet culture has infiltrated health and education, so the food rules start younger and younger. But as many parents know, children aren't always happy to follow the rules – no matter how many well-intentioned leaflets they bring home from school.

If food stresses you out it's no wonder, and if it's starting to stress your kids out then that's no wonder either. How can we expect children to be in tune with their bodies when all these external rules and complicated emotional layers are being placed around eating and mealtimes? It's no longer enough just to 'Eat up'. Our kids now have to 'Eat up, avoid that, only have one of those and make sure you have this too'. And, quite frankly, it's exhausting.

Giving up the food micromanagement

The way we approach our kids' feeding is often informed by our own attitude to food. This attitude will have been borne from our own experiences as kids, our exposure to harmful diet culture messages, the society we live in and the marketing around food and health that we've absorbed throughout our life. And, without realising it, we can sometimes end up falling into a trap of micromanaging what the children in our care eat based on some of these attitudes – and I'm not just talking *what* we feed them but also *how* we feed them.

Many dieticians and nutritionists are moving away from the diet culture mentality as the health risks of dieting and the benefits of the HAES paradigm (see page 88) become more widely known. Two such dieticians are US-based Evelyn Tribole and Elyse Resch, who pioneered a new approach to nutrition called 'intuitive eating' in their book of the same name, originally published in 1995 and now in its fourth edition.[1] Their work has led to more than 125 studies showing the benefits of the approach and over 1,100 certified intuitive eating counsellors around the world.

Intuitive eating is about honouring your natural hunger and fullness cues – cues which many experts argue most of us are born with and only need to relearn as adults after external rules see us lose connection with them. It might be that we've lost this inbuilt ability through dieting, or it might be that as kids we lost the ability to regulate our own appetites because we were constantly being told what and how much to eat.

There are ten principles to intuitive eating, which include rejecting the diet mentality, challenging the food police and respecting your body. Much of the advice in this chapter is developed from the knowledge around intuitive eating and a HAES approach to nutrition, which, as we heard in Chapter 3, is about recognising and celebrating body diversity and giving up the diet rules that tell us you can only be healthy (or beautiful) if your body looks a certain way.

It might be unclear how this relates to children, but when you think back to your childhood when you were told by an adult not to eat too much of something or to eat more of something else, then the pieces of the puzzle start to come together. Many of the rules adults use to police children's food come from the belief that big = bad and that big can be avoided by cutting out certain foods or eating more of others.

Registered nutritionist Sarah Dempster says these rules can erode our children's ability to eat intuitively. 'If we observe a baby once milk feeding is established, we can usually recognise the signals that they are hungry, and once they are full they usually lose interest in the milk,' says Sarah. 'But sometimes we pressure them to have a certain amount of milk or a fixed number of feeds – this can begin to undermine their ability to eat intuitively. Pressure to "finish your plate" often continues through childhood, along with other things that undermine children's ability to connect to what their bodies need, from offering certain foods as "treats" or rewards, to the way that food is marketed, to the messages children absorb from diet culture. Some of this is impossible to avoid in our current culture, but parents and caregivers can help children by creating a supportive environment at home.'

We have got so hung up on what is and isn't healthy, and the need to stick to these rules in order to be good parents and raise healthy children that, ironically, we may be introducing them to some pretty unhealthy eating tendencies. We've made things too complicated, too stressful and taken the joy out of food. Eating can be a time for a family to come together and celebrate. It can be a bonding experience as well as a chance to fuel your body with energy. Food can be straightforward and happy, and most kids are born with the ability to know this instinctively.

'When children are pushed to eat something they don't want to, this teaches them they can't trust their own body,' explains Sarah. 'This counts for amounts as well as types of food. So, for example, if we set an expectation for a child to finish their plate or bottle, they learn to eat according to an external cue (the empty plate) rather than what their body needs. This may mean they eat past the point of fullness and get used to eating more than they actually need. If we pressure children to eat a food they don't like or are unfamiliar with (and this can even apply to gentler forms of pressure such as encouragement and praise), it can backfire too. Some children may eat the food simply to please their parent or caregiver, while others will double down and refuse to ever try that food.'

The other side of the coin is restriction. Remember that time I was scolded for not eating everything on my plate at a play date? This house also had a 'treat cupboard'. The treat cupboard was the top shelf of a kitchen cupboard that only the parents in the house could reach and it was stuffed to bursting with every type of biscuit and chocolate bar that a seven-year-old could hope to eat. As I recall, when you opened the door a beautiful golden light would shine and angels would start singing.

The 'treat cupboard' was only reserved for those who 'finished their plate' and was 100 per cent not for little hands to help themselves to. And because of this added layer of mystery, the chocolate bars inside tasted even more special.

This attitude to sweets and snacks isn't uncommon, says Sarah. But while we think restricting our kids' access to these types of foods is about protecting their health, this type of approach can cause problems. 'Children who feel like their access to sweets and snacks is restricted, or disapproved of, tend to eat more when presented with free access to those foods, and also tend to feel more negatively about their eating. Some studies suggest that restriction can also make food advertising more appealing. So, essentially, by trying to control the amount and type of food that children eat, we move them away from tuning into their bodies' needs and instead set them up to take more of their eating cues from their external environment.'

Hearing all this might be setting off alarm bells in your head. You might also have a treat cupboard and you might encourage your kids to eat up their vegetables. And if you do, you need to know that you're not alone. In fact, one study found that 85 per cent of parents used varying strategies to encourage their kids to eat, with pressure, praise and reward all common tactics.[2] These habits are so deeply ingrained that we are almost preconditioned to approach food in this way around children. But the alternative doesn't have to be scary. In fact, the alternative is a whole lot less stressful than the micromanagement approach. Remember, it's not too late – change is possible.

IT'S NOT ALL ON YOU

Intuitive eating is a practice that allows us to have a peaceful, rule-free attitude towards food and our bodies. There are entire books written on this approach, but one of the key things to take away is that it is about trusting your body – or relearning to trust your body's innate knowledge for how and what it wants to eat. This can take time and work for adults to figure out, and to move away from the diet mentality, food rules and ideas of 'good' and 'bad' food learned over a lifetime. If you've ever been to a festival and eaten fried food for three days straight then craved a salad, that's your body telling you that it knows what it wants. And this is where things get interesting, because if we can trust our own bodies to relearn this, then we need to trust our kids' bodies to know this already.

This is where Ellyn Satter's 'Division of Responsibility in Feeding' (or sDOR) comes in.[3] Ellyn Satter is an internationally renowned family therapist and feeding and eating specialist, a registered dietician and the author of multiple bestselling books on children and feeding. 'Satter's work is a trust model – the idea that we, as parents, trust our children to eat the amount of food that is right for them. In turn children trust us that they are going to be fed at regular times throughout the day,' explains Sarah Dempster, who uses the sDOR model in her own work. 'It's important to acknowledge that this looks different for different children – diversity in appetite is normal. To help children maintain their innate ability to eat what they need once they start solid foods, Satter recommends adults take responsibility for the *what, when* and *where* of feeding. Children are then responsible for the *how much* and the *whether* of eating.'

What does this look like in real life? It means that, as the adult, you are responsible for providing the food. You can choose what to buy at the supermarket, what to cook for dinner, as well as when and where you'll eat it. After this though, it's on the kids.

Many experts agree that it's best to have at least one of the day's meals around the table together as a family, and to have a routine around when this will be so you're not eating at completely different times every day.[4] Eating together as a family not only provides a good opportunity to role model eating behaviour for children, but it also conveys cultural traditions. What's more, evidence also shows a strong link between children and teens who eat regularly with their family and higher academic attainment (yes, really!).[5] And there are some studies which show eating together as a family can be good for children's psychological functioning and even lead to teens being less likely to engage in risk-taking behaviours like drinking alcohol.[6]

'At this point, children can decide not to eat, to only eat certain foods, or to eat everything and ask for another helping,' says Sarah. 'Once this structure is in place, the emphasis is on making mealtimes enjoyable and trusting kids to do their thing. Children's appetites fluctuate and it's normal for them to eat a lot at some meals and very little at others. The important things are that your children get the opportunity to try the foods their parents eat, that they're able to choose the amount they want to eat, that there's some predictable structure to meal timings, and that they get the social benefits of eating with other people. Beyond this, individual circumstances vary and it's important to make it work for you and your family, and seek support from a health professional early on if you have any concerns about your child's eating.' Problems with eating can show up in a range of ways and there are various behavioural, physical and psychological symptoms that can signify an issue. A whole chapter could be devoted to this alone, but, essentially, if you are concerned then seek help. Trusting your child's ability to feed themselves does not mean you can't get reassurance from a health professional if you are worried about something.

The Resources section at the end of this book will give you guidance on where to find support (page 233).

I realise the idea of trusting in kids' eating intuition is sometimes easier said than done. There is nothing more frustrating than spending hours sweating over a meal only for your kids to take one look at it and push their plates away. I know; I've been there.

My youngest daughter is what many would describe as a 'picky eater' (researchers now prefer the terms 'selective' or 'choosy') and there have been many family meals where I've silently screamed on the inside as she's refused to eat what's in front of her. But the sDOR model has really helped take the conflict out of mealtimes for us. This approach made me see that sometimes I was putting too much on my daughter's plate and she was simply overwhelmed with what was in front of her, so we started having more meals where she would serve herself. I realised this one Christmas when I put all the elements of the roast dinner on the table and she served her own vegetables and ate most of them happily. (We made sure not to praise her or even comment on it, which proved tougher than it might sound!)

The sDOR tool also helped me realise that, in my daughter's case, some of her refusal to eat came from wanting to be in control. And I realised that it made sense – if someone was telling me to eat every pea on my plate I'd probably want to just throw them all on the floor too. When you're five and you don't have a huge amount of control over much in your life, the one thing you can be in charge of is how much you eat. This is another important lesson in consent, I think.

If the thought of giving up pressuring your kids to eat their veg brings you out in a cold sweat, you might be interested to know that many studies show pressuring kids to eat certain foods has no impact on whether they eat that food or not, on their weight or on their food choices generally.[7] And a 2020 study showed that the more parents pressure their picky eaters, the more 'finicky' they may become.[8] Studies also show that pressuring children to eat food they don't like can create tension and negatively impact the parent–child relationship. Researchers found this out in a 2018 study in Michigan when they examined a group of toddlers over a year and found that their weight remained stable on growth charts, whether they were so-called picky eaters or not, and that pressuring the children to eat didn't stop them being picky eaters.[9] This confirms that, as parents, we have a lot to lose but very little to gain by making mealtimes a battleground and pressuring our kids to eat every last (or any) scrap of broccoli on their plate.

Another thing to remember is that, just like adults, kids' appetites will vary day to day. And it's also very normal for kids to change their mind over what they like to eat. If you're tearing your hair out because your child won't eat their peas today, know that tomorrow this might not be the case. Psychologists have long since known about the 'theory of habituation' – that the more you encounter something, the less likely you are to react to it. And child feeding specialists say this is true for kids and food too. The more children are exposed to a food, the more comfortable they will feel around it.

This counts both for the foods you might be keen for your kids to eat lots of and the ones you'd rather they avoid. So, if your child turns their nose up at their vegetables today, keep offering them tomorrow. The more they see veg and become used to it, the more likely they are to feel comfortable around it and choose to eat it. In fact, evidence shows it can take up to 15 times of being exposed to a food before a child will accept it.[10]

And, by the same token, don't ban sweets or put anything with sugar under lock and key either. Experts warn that if children never see sweets or cake or ice cream at home, then the more likely they are to lose all control around these foods on the rare occasions they do get a chance to eat them.[11] Simply taking away the 'treat' mentality around these types of foods is a good place to start, which means avoiding using sweets as a reward or punishment – and that includes not persuading your kids to eat all their dinner in order to get dessert.

In fact, the sDOR model takes it a step further, advocating for parents to regularly include foods that are high in fat and sugar, in unlimited amounts, during regular, structured, sit-down snack times, to give children the opportunity to learn to moderate their consumption of these types of food in a structured setting. Avoiding demonising these foods or giving them a special 'treat' status will both reduce the risk of kids developing a 'deprivation mindset' around these types of food and mean they are more likely to have a longer-lasting happy relationship with food.

This is where we come to the next piece of the happy eating puzzle for kids: the importance of keeping it neutral and giving up food labels which put some foods on a pedestal and relegate others to the bottom of the pile.

KEEP IT NEUTRAL

The idea that 'You are what you eat' isn't a new one – food and morality have gone together since the beginning of time. Arguably the most famous story in the Bible is about someone eating something they shouldn't; Eve committing the first sin of humankind by eating an apple is a clear portrayal of how food, virtue and sin are linked in our collective cultural consciousness.

Religious professor Alan Levinovitz summarised the link between food and morality in an interview with Rachel Sugar for Vox.com in 2018 when he said: 'The way we create identity for ourselves is – in part, at least – through rituals, and the ritual of eating is a really important one. We have to do it three times a day, it's very personal, we take something from outside of our bodies and put it inside of our bodies, so it makes sense that we would really pay attention to that ritual as something that helps us to articulate our values.'[12]

Just as the Evangelical Protestant movement that we learned about in Chapter 2 made connections between the food someone eats and their religious upstanding and value as a good citizen (see page 47), we've now come full circle to a time where our moral worth and value as productive, useful members of society is equated with what we eat – except these days health has replaced religion as the signifier of worth. And, interestingly, many of the words we now use to describe food carry religious and moral undertones too. Whether it's 'cheat days' or if your food is 'clean', the message is clear: some food is good and, by association, you are a good person if you eat it, while some is bad and, by association, you are a bad person if you eat it.

What is all this teaching our children? Children don't have the cognitive resources to untangle the nuance of language. They think about things in binary, black-and-white terms. If you tell a child a food is 'good' they will believe that food is good – and that the person eating it is also good. And vice versa if we tell a child a food is 'bad'. The same is true for labels like 'healthy' and 'unhealthy'. But, in reality, food is just food. Sure, some food is more nutrient-dense than others, but this does not mean it should be placed on a pedestal, that we should vilify anyone who doesn't eat it or that you are a more worthy, better, morally upright person if you eat it. Eating kale does not automatically make you a good person and eating chocolate does not automatically make you a bad one. We need to take the guilt, shame and praise away from food, and we can only do this if we start using neutral language around it.

Shana Spence is a registered dietician nutritionist based in New York who runs the platform The Nutrition Tea. 'I use an "all foods fit" approach to nutrition. Instead of saying "I can't have this food because it has too much sugar", I suggest saying "It's OK to enjoy this and I know to add in more vegetables and fruits to my next meal". It's all about mentality and how to change our way of thinking. We need to start teaching children there are no such things as "good" and "bad" foods. Different foods will provide you with different nutrients. Yes – even sugar, which will give you energy. And your body needs carbohydrates (it's the main fuel for our brain). We should be looking at food as fuel and not demonising certain foods and categories. This way of thinking is important for our mental health as well.'

And it's not just about neutral language. We also need to create neutral environments too. This means avoiding the praise and pressure that we've just heard about and reducing any opportunity for tension at the table.

This will have huge benefits for children both at home and at school. Not only will they be less likely to crave the 'bad' foods, they'll be more likely to try the 'good' ones too. And also, they'll be less likely to judge other kids who they see

eating the 'bad' foods. This is very important when we take into account the food landscape that we live in, and the fact that many families don't have as easy access to the nutrient-dense food that is often put on a pedestal by non-neutral language and environments. We'll hear more about this in a minute.

As you're reading this, you might be rolling your eyes, thinking, 'But how will I teach my kids about food?!' Please don't get me wrong. I am not saying you can't teach the children in your care about food. I am not saying you shouldn't get kids involved in helping to prepare food or grow food. I am not saying you shouldn't encourage your kids to learn where food comes from or be amazed at the wonder of a vegetable growing from a tiny seed in the ground. This stuff is fun and joyous and interesting, and it is absolutely not off limits. And, what's more, evidence shows that it will create a much better foundation for a long-lasting happy and healthy relationship with food for kids in the future.[13] Remember the theory of habituation we talked about earlier? There's no better way to get used to food than growing it from seed and then turning it into a tasty meal (see page 146 for more on this).

FOOD, CHILDREN AND SOCIETY (IT'S ALL ABOUT THE MONEY)

We can't talk about raising happy eaters without at least acknowledging the socioeconomic factors involved in eating and how the food landscape that we live in impacts our eating choices. This is what this next section is about. Pay particular attention here if you've ever made a judgement about another parent for the food they feed their children, or fallen into the trap of thinking all kids have the same access to nutritious meals.

Between 2018 and 2019 The Trussell Trust in the UK handed out 1.6 million food parcels and warned that food bank use had risen by 73 per cent in the past five years.[14] In April 2020 they reported an 89 per cent rise in food bank use in their networks, compared with April 2019, and a 107 per cent rise in food parcels for children.[15] Their 18-month research project with the University of Oxford (the single biggest nationwide study in the UK on food bank use to date) found that 78 per cent of the 400 households involved in the survey were severely food insecure, regularly skipping meals and going without eating, sometimes for days at a time.[16] Twenty-five per cent of those surveyed blamed rising food expenses, showing the impact of food inflation on squeezed budgets.

In 2018 the Social Market Foundation released a report claiming that 10.2 million people in Great Britain live in a 'food desert', which they defined as an area poorly served by food stores.[17] The report also showed that high and unaffordable food prices have led to 38 per cent of households shopping in cheaper food stores and 23 per cent buying cheaper, less nutrient-dense food, and that smaller convenience stores may charge a premium for some items compared with larger supermarkets.

It's a similar picture in the US. The US Department of Agriculture counted 11 million children living with hunger at the last count, and approximately 23.5 million people living in food deserts.[18] They also estimate 2.3 million people in the US live in low-income rural areas more than 10 miles from a supermarket. A 2006 study also found that people living in the poorest areas of the US have two-and-a-half times the exposure to fast-food restaurants as those living in the wealthiest areas.[19]

It's more complex than just proximity to a supermarket though. In a 2018 interview with *Guernica* magazine, food justice activist Karen Washington argued to move away from the term 'food desert' in favour of 'food apartheid' to take into account the systemic racism permeating America's food system.[20] Speaking with writer Anna Brones, she said: 'In my neighbourhood there is a fast-food restaurant on every block. Now drugstores are popping up on every corner, too. So you have the fast-food restaurants that of course cause the diet-related diseases, and you have the pharmaceutical companies there to fix it. They go hand in hand. The fact is, if you do prevention, someone is going to lose money. If you give people access to really good food and a living-wage job, someone is going to lose money. As long as people are poor and as long as people are sick, there are jobs to be made. Follow the money . . . "Food apartheid" looks at the whole food system, along with race, geography, faith and economics. You say "food apartheid" and you get to the root cause of some of the problems around the food system.'

I haven't even touched on the food industry and regulation, or how food politics and market forces impact what we eat. Just like the diet industry is worth billions worldwide, so is the food industry, and it makes good business sense to persuade us to eat heavily processed foods that aren't as high in nutrients as the less marketed original food sources. What's more, there's strong evidence to show that the majority of foods children see in marketing and advertising are high in fat, sugar and salt (the official term for these are 'HFSS foods'), and this can affect kids' preferences and the things they ask their parents to buy.[21] The food industry has to take some responsibility here too. Food, just like everything else, is political.

Access to nutritious food isn't the only issue though – having the time and equipment to prepare food is another privilege. If you're working long hours on a low income you might struggle both to find the time to buy the ingredients in your budget and to use them to cook a meal from scratch.

While there's not a huge amount you can do as one person reading this right now, knowing this information might help you question some of the regular 'food police'-type assertions that are so normalised they often go unchallenged. And the more people who are aware these issues exist, the higher chance we have collectively of fighting for *all* children to have the basics needed to be raised as happy eaters.

How to Take the Conflict out of Mealtimes

The science

Everything in this toolkit is based on what you've just read, on the theories around losing the food rules, the sDOR, the theory of habituation, neutrality, as well as the evidence behind the impact of role modelling on children.

Research shows that environment and food-related experiences are central to the development of how children eat, and that preferences formed early on in life tend to continue into adulthood.[22] So creating a relaxed eating environment isn't just conducive to raising happy eaters now but later on too.

This guide is not meant as an alternative set of rules to follow, rather a series of guidelines to help you find out what works for your family when it comes to food and eating. Think of it as a gentle nudge of encouragement to help take the conflict out of food and remove some of the stress around family mealtimes.

Most importantly, know that while some of these suggestions might sound easy on paper, in practice they might take a bit of work to get used to. We don't unlearn a lifetime of habits overnight and, as we've already discussed, much of our attitude to feeding and kids comes from what we learned ourselves as children or the rules we've internalised around food throughout our own life.

You might also find that changing your mindset around how you feed your kids could bring up unresolved issues around food for yourself. If this is the case, you may want to explore these feelings in a supportive environment and you'll find resources to help with this at the end of book (see page 233).

The tool: a happy eating guide for kids

Bookmark this page and refer to it whenever you need a quick reminder of ways to take the conflict out of mealtimes. As you use these guidelines more and more, some of them will become second nature. Remember, a bad mealtime does not make you a bad parent, so if things don't go well today then start again tomorrow. Be as gentle on yourself with this stuff as you are on your kids – food is joy and connection and fuel and celebration. This is your chance to take the happy bits of food and lose the negativity.

You can use this guide at any stage of your child's development and wherever you are – at home, on holiday or in a restaurant.

Warning words

Remember how we learned the power of neutral language on food (see page 135)? Here's a list of words to watch out for when talking about food and eating with kids and teenagers.

Avoid all the words in both of these columns if you can:

Bad	Good
Sinful	Sin-free
Cheat	Strict
Unhealthy	Healthy
High-calorie	Low-calorie
Dirty	Clean
Naughty	Nice
Treat	Being good
Guilty pleasure	Guilt-free

Use basic descriptors instead – a fruit smoothie is just a fruit smoothie, not a 'healthy, guilt-free, good' fruit smoothie. And a biscuit is just a biscuit, not a 'treat' or 'guilty pleasure'.

The power of the family meal
It doesn't need to be a long, drawn-out dinner. Twenty to thirty minutes together as a family is enough, around five times a week, and it could be for breakfast or lunch, not necessarily an evening meal. It does need to be together though, and away from the TV. Evidence shows that eating while watching TV isn't just bad for conversation, it can even inhibit digestion and lead us to lose connection with our appetite because we're distracted from the process of eating.[23]

Self-service
Giving young children the chance to serve themselves is a great way to let them take control over how much they eat and what is on their plate. If you're serving up yourself then try offering smaller portions and giving the chance for kids to have more if they want it, instead of overloading their plate.

Release the pressure

Once you're at the table, lose the pressure. Avoid food bargaining, encouragement, bribery or threats. This is an important part of the sDOR model and it might feel strange at first because these habits can be so ingrained. Remember, it's your job to provide the food but it's your child's job to decide whether to eat it.

Because this stuff dies hard, here are some phrases to watch out for:

» 'Eat it all up or you won't have pudding.'
» 'Clear your plate.'
» 'Just three [or however many] more mouthfuls.'
» 'Well done for eating those peas!'

If you're with other family members, such as grandparents, talk to them beforehand about your approach and explain why you're doing it so your kids don't encounter food policing elsewhere. This can be a tough one because often children can experience food bargaining in school. If you're worried about this, you might like to talk to your child's school or put a note in their lunchbox letting teachers know your wishes. If this is something you want to do, here's a template you can use:

Dear _____

We are raising _____ to be a happy eater. Part of this is to trust them to know what and how much they want to eat. Please allow _____ to decide how much, and in what order, they want to eat their lunch. I trust that _____ knows their own appetite. If you have any questions please feel free to contact me on _____. Thank you for looking after _____, we appreciate your support with this.

Get growing

We talked about the theory of habituation earlier and the power of teaching kids about where food comes from, so getting children involved in growing food is a great way to encourage them to become familiar with food. There's even evidence to show growing food together can lead to children being more interested in eating vegetables.[24] Plus, as we've already found out, gardening is a brilliant mindfulness activity (self-care – tick!) and it's good for body image too.

Get them involved

Children, regardless of their age, can benefit from getting hands-on with food. Encouraging kids to be involved in the preparation of food is a bonding experience as well as an opportunity for them to get used to the food (it's that theory of habituation thing again). Even very young children will benefit from exploring food – touching it, smelling it and getting used to how it feels. As much as you may hate the mess, it's great if you can encourage an open-door policy in the kitchen and make it a place that isn't out of bounds. Do this, though, without the expectation that this will mean your child will necessarily eat the food that they have helped prepare. There are many benefits from getting hands-on with food, so long as the you don't have a hidden (or not-so-hidden) agenda.

CHAPTER 6

Making Movement Fun Again

Walk past any school playground at break time and you'll likely see a variety of children doing a variety of different things. Some will be playing football, some will be dancing, some will be whispering to each other in a corner, some will be playing chase.

The school playground is a prime example of children's natural ability to embrace joyful movement. They rest when they're tired and run about when they're energetic. I've never once walked past my daughters' playground at break time and seen a group of kids doing burpees or squats while shouting, 'Feel the burn! No pain no gain!' And it's rare to see a child walk when they can hop, skip and jump instead. For children, movement is natural and exercise is intuitive, fun and just a part of life.

This chapter will give you the tools to keep it that way. Just like diet culture has messed up our relationship with food, it's also messed up our relationship with exercise. We've learned to associate movement with punishment and with something we 'should' do to keep our bodies in line. But it should be fun, joyful, spontaneous, just a part of life.

Diet culture has ruined exercise

In the last chapter we learned how making formal rules around food can unlearn our children's natural intuition when it comes to their appetite. The same is true of exercise. As soon as we start placing moral judgements around movement, not only do we risk excluding some children, we also risk losing the fun.

Disclaimer: I was always a fairly sporty kid. I loved swimming, did a lot of dance and really enjoyed athletics and cross-country at secondary school. But by the time I reached university I'd pretty much stopped doing any movement, unless it involved burning a specific number of calories or getting 'ripped', because I thought it was a waste of time. Ironically, I was president of the Yoga Society at uni (what?! It's a thing!), but viewed my weekly yoga session as 'relaxation' and didn't equate the movement I did during the class as 'proper' exercise.

Diet culture is so ingrained in fitness that, at some point along the way, I stopped listening to my body and stopped moving it for how it made me feel, choosing instead to prioritise movement as a tool to change my body shape. The beginning of viewing exercise in this way also marked the beginning of an erratic and unhealthy relationship with movement. Instead of consistently moving my body because I enjoyed it, I'd go through spurts of activity only to give up after a couple of weeks.

Sunday evenings would usually be spent planning all the workouts I needed to do to make up for the fun I'd had over the weekend (and by fun I mean all the food and drink I'd consumed on 'cheat days'). And Monday mornings would often see me hauling my tired body out of bed before putting it through a punishing workout that I hated every second of.

Sometimes I'd keep up the pattern of movement for a few weeks, hoping that forced continuity would spark some kind of enthusiasm. But more often than not I'd give up after a couple of days, berate myself, feel guilty and like a failure, and then tell myself I'd start again when I was ready to begin whatever new form of diet and fitness punishment was needed before a holiday, or Christmas, or whatever event I told myself I needed to 'get in shape' for.

For me, fitness was always something I did when I wanted to change my body, when I felt uncomfortable in my skin. No matter how much I told myself it was about 'getting healthy' or a 'lifestyle change', my main motivation for movement was to shrink, tone and shape my body. It was certainly not about celebrating what my body could do or enjoying how it made me feel.

My experience is not uncommon. Research shows that exercising for appearance-based motivations is associated with poor body image and low self-esteem,[1] while studies also show that those who exercise for health and enjoyment are more likely to have a positive body image.[2] And in yet another twist in why our bodies are amazing, the science also shows that your motivation for exercise can even impact the benefit it has on your body. In 2007 researchers reported that people who were motivated to exercise for health and enjoyment reasons had lower pulse rates, systolic blood pressure and salivary stress hormone levels, while those who were motivated by weight loss had none of these physical improvements.[3]

I continued this approach when I had children, and while I was crying through a burpee or forcing my sleep-deprived body into a plank, my kids were watching. I was showing them that exercise was something to endure, something to force yourself to do and definitely, *definitely*, not fun. I wasn't exactly a walking advert for the joys of movement.

You might not think this matters, but the science says otherwise. A study in 2016 across five different European countries found that maternal, but not paternal, participation in sport, outdoor activities and walking for transport were associated with higher participation in these activities in children, showing that children learn through role modelling.[4] This study makes for positive reading, because it shows if we can sort out our own attitudes to movement then there's hope for our kids.

These days I no longer exercise to change my body. And the irony is that I now exercise consistently, regularly and – most importantly – I love it. When I decided to give up dieting, I gave up pushing my body through gruelling regimes that I hated and dedicated my time to finding types of movement that I looked forward to doing. I remembered my university yoga days and began doing yoga again – realising it was about way more than just relaxation. I started running and began regularly running long routes through the countryside, often listening to a podcast while I ran. And I discovered the joy of a kitchen disco.

Then, in 2019, I slipped a disc in my back while camping (the glamour!), permanently damaging the disc and narrowly avoiding surgery. I spent the summer on crutches and it was then that I realised how much I'd come to rely on movement as a general mood-booster and stress-reliever, how much exercise made me appreciate my body, and how all those years of forcing myself to do workouts that I hated were wasted. My back is still damaged, and it will be forever. I can no longer run with wild abandon through fields, but I can swim and do yoga and gentle weights and have – after 20 years – finally found a gym I love. I'm there at 6.30am most weekdays and can honestly say it's a highlight of each day. My body hasn't changed shape – if anything it's softer and rounder – but I am 100 per cent healthier and have a healthier attitude to movement. And, most importantly, I'm role modelling this attitude to my kids.

INTRODUCING INTUITIVE MOVEMENT

Intuitive movement, or joyful movement, is about giving up the diet culture rules around fitness and moving your body for pleasure. If, like me, you've spent most of your life viewing exercise as a punishment or a way to mould your body, looking at exercise in this way can require a radical mindset shift. But if we want to show our kids the joys of movement, then it's important.

'The main outcome of adopting an intuitive approach to fitness is about finding a way of engaging with movement that has longevity, is sustainable and is something you look forward to doing, rather than feeling like it's a punishing thing you have to do to control and manipulate your body,' explains fitness trainer and author of the book *Train Happy*, Tally Rye. 'It's an extension of Health at Every Size, because it's about focusing on encouraging health-promoting behaviours and saying that weight is not a behaviour. While we *can't* control our body size we *can* enhance the way we feel, which means using exercise as a form of self-care and a tool to feel good, as opposed to punishment and weight control.'

There are many benefits of looking at movement in this way, but perhaps the biggest is that, as we've just found out, exercising for intrinsic reasons (how it makes us feel) leads to

a more consistent relationship with movement than exercising for extrinsic reasons (how it makes us look). Teaching kids that exercise is about these things now could set them up for a lifetime of joyful movement later.

'The way we internalise what exercise is as adults can get absorbed by children so they learn, for example, that if their tummy is getting big they should do some exercise,' says Tally. 'But I think we need to adopt a more holistic approach and help children realise what their bodies are capable of doing and talk about these benefits using positive language and reinforcement so that kids internalise these ideas instead. Talk to them about how exercise impacts their mood, ask them to think about how they feel when they play and expend energy. These are hugely formative years and we can get a lot of push-back in later life if people have bad memories of movement and what it meant to them as a child. Ultimately we want to keep people active for as long as possible, so rather than "go hard and go strong", emphasise play, enjoyment and fun, and create environments where those things can happen regularly and consistently, without adding moral value to movement.'

The chances are that your children already practise joyful movement without even thinking about it, in which case maybe you need to simply follow their lead. This can be a really great opportunity to learn from children about what they find fun and trusting their intuition to do these things. It can also be a brilliant bonding activity. A family bike ride, a game of Twister, jumping around trying to pop some indoor bubbles, taking up roller skating or skateboarding, learning some tricks on a stunt scooter … these are all chances to try out different types of movement and find something you enjoy while also giving your kids access to these activities too.

If you're still not convinced of the benefits of movement without aesthetics as the motivator, then you might be interested to know that exercise can boost self-esteem, relieve stress, increase strength and stamina, give increased sensitivity to hunger and fullness, help prevent against injury and aid better sleep, to name just a few things. Movement can be an end in itself; it doesn't have to be a route towards something else. It can be fun and joyful, a family bonding activity, a chance to try new things. It doesn't need to be something we do to 'get healthy', to 'bulk up', to lose weight, or something we do because we 'should'.

MOVEMENT FOR EVERY BODY

Diet culture tells us that not only is exercise something to do to make or keep your body thin, but exercise is only for people who want to become or stay thin. There's an assumption that if you have a fat body you don't work out. Ironically, when the opposite is proved to be true, and people in bigger bodies do work out, it can make some people angry because it challenges what they believe to be true about fatness and fitness.

In 2019 Nike put a plus-size mannequin in their London store and it caused uproar. 'This mannequin promotes obesity!' screamed the headlines.[5] At the time it seemed ironic to me that the same people who shout 'Fat people just need to do some exercise' were the ones advocating for people in bigger bodies not to have access to gear which allows them to work out, and not to see representation which might encourage them to take part in exercise in the first place.

It's also ironic because the science proves this notion of fatness and fitness to be wrong. Evidence shows that people who are fat and fit live longer than those who are thin and unfit.[6] Despite what diet culture tells us, it's the fitness, not the body size, which is the key.

In many fitness spaces though, these messages aren't getting through. Part of the problem is that fitness professionals are often scrutinised for their bodies and, in turn, perpetuate anti-fat ideas on to others (this was shown in a 2017 study).[7] And part of the problem is that the way fitness is sold to us is still as a tool to lose weight. But studies show that fitness spaces that emphasise appearance and weight loss are related to higher self-objectification (bad for body image, remember?!),[8] while function-focused comments, such as 'look at how strong you're getting', by fitness instructors can improve mood and body appreciation.[9] What's more, research shows children who experience criticism of their weight have negative attitudes to sport and are less likely to engage in exercise.[10] So making movement about weight loss is turning people *off* exercise, not encouraging them to do it.

When we perpetuate the idea that movement is just for aesthetics or that anyone with a bigger body doesn't work out, we risk alienating many children from exercise and setting them up to live a lifetime in conflict with movement. You might think that kids don't pick up on these messages, but my experience online shows this isn't the case.

'Obese children need to do more exercise!'; 'Fat kids shouldn't be fat – they need to do some sport!'; 'Their parents should make them lose weight and work out!' are some of the comments I regularly get on Instagram about children and body acceptance. And many of the people posting these comments are teenage boys.

When you hear these types of comments it's perhaps unsurprising that stats show that 36 per cent of girls and 24 per cent of boys regularly avoid exercise and PE due to worries about appearance.[11] These kids are not just hearing that fitness looks one way from the media, they're getting it from their own classmates, who are probably getting it from wider society and possibly their own parents and teachers too. And so the cycle continues.

In fact, there are various studies to show that PE teachers themselves could be part of the problem.[12] (If you're a PE teacher reading this right now, please don't take offence – I'm not saying you do this, but it might be useful to look at the culture in your department and see if any of this rings true. If we want to engage kids in exercise, we need to be aware of some of the attitudes getting in the way of their love of movement in the first place.) In 2007 researchers did a study into anti-fat bias in physical educators and found that PE teachers expressed worse attitudes compared to teachers of other subjects.[13] They also found that those training to be PE teachers believed strongly that larger kids lacked willpower, with the teachers nearer the end of their training expressing stronger weight bias than those at the start, despite taking formal classes on 'the causes of obesity'. Other work also found that PE teachers perceived children in bigger bodies to have poorer social, reasoning, physical and cooperation skills.[14] And in another study researchers found that kids are not immune to these attitudes – the children in the study reported negative comments from teachers around weight and said it led to them avoiding PE.[15]

Plus-size athlete, author and fitness business founder Louise Green is one of the voices challenging these limiting ideas of exercise, and her book *Big Fit Girl* is a rallying cry for wider representation and inclusivity in fitness spaces.[16] Louise highlights the importance of changing the discourse around fitness and showing that people of size are just as capable of being exceptional athletes as those in smaller bodies.

'The imagery and the messaging we put around fitness is the unspoken invitation,' says Louise. 'When people can't see a likeness to themselves, then people think "That's not for me". The amount of fear that is around fitness for a lot of people is intense, and I think if we can start instilling those messages and images very early on, and younger people see a range of body sizes and ages and ethnicities and abilities, then they'll start to see themselves in that message and want to participate.'

Louise knows this from experience, because her own relationship with exercise changed forever when she started training for her first 5k and met a plus-size running coach. 'I thought that if I just started running I'd look like the people on the cover of the magazines; I thought it was my ticket to thinness,' says Louise. 'I went to this clinic, petrified, and our leader stood up and introduced herself, and she was a plus-size woman. At that time Facebook was only just starting to gain momentum and Instagram didn't exist, so I'd never seen images of people like me as a runner or in fitness leadership. And I'd never seen a woman that was just running and leading people to run in the body she had, without there being weight loss attached to it.'

For Louise, seeing another person of size enjoy exercise in a non-diet culture context was the beginning of a whole new life. 'That was when I really started to appreciate my body for what it can do and where it can take me, not how it looked,' says Louise. 'And I think that's a really great message for kids because, as we grow, and if our bodies are not doing what we want them to do, there can be this mind–body disconnection, and I think physical movement really pulls that together, and it builds confidence too. That's why it's not just about fitness for me, it's about feeling your power, feeling self-confident, feeling like you can take on the world.'

All movement is valid

One of the keys to discovering a happy relationship with movement is to remember that all movement is valid. This is also a really important part of making movement inclusive for all children – not just the sporty ones – and to giving kids the tools to move their bodies in a way that feels good for them on any given day. You do not *have* to 'go hard or go home'.

When we view exercise through a diet culture context – or even through an educational context – and prioritise some forms of movement over others, we risk creating value judgements and rules which can get in the way of allowing children to discover what they enjoy. Football is great, sure, but so is a fun afternoon trying to recreate the dance moves on your kids' favourite pop music video or TikTok account. Netball is brilliant, but so is some gentle stretching in a kids' yoga class. A trip to the beach or to the park can provide lots of opportunities for movement which are just as valid as a formal PE session or dance class. All movement is good movement and all bodies are good bodies.

Remember in the last chapter we talked about taking the morality away from food and not placing some food on a pedestal (see page 137)? The same is true of movement. There are lots of different types of movement, and with each form of exercise comes a different benefit. Competitive sport was prized 150 years ago by schools to prepare young people (particularly boys) for 'the rigours of life'. This stopped in the eighties over fears it was damaging to less sporty kids. But in recent years competitive sport has made a comeback as educators see the role it can play in building resilience in children and giving them the chance to experience the emotions that come with winning and losing in a 'peer environment'. These benefits should be open to all children of all shapes and sizes. Stereotypes that promote certain activities as requiring a particular body type immediately exclude any child without that shape from taking part. Get rid of the body ideal, widen the representation, and the door immediately opens to more children to engage with that form of movement.

There are lots of pluses to competitive sport that have nothing to do with the movement itself – including learning to work as a team and gaining self-confidence. And sport generally can be a really great way for children to learn about discipline, as well as an opportunity to meet new friends. But organised sports are not the only way to get children engaged with movement – and if your kids are not into formal sport activities there are plenty of other ways they can find joy in moving their bodies.

Donna Noble is a yoga specialist, intuitive well-being coach and founder of CurveSome Yoga. As well as a body-positive class, she also teaches aqua yoga, postnatal yoga and accessible yoga alongside vinyasa flow, hot yoga and chair yoga. She believes that parents shouldn't underestimate the power of yoga – and even if your kids love football, there is benefit in introducing them to yoga too.

'Movement is key and if you don't use it you lose it,' says Donna. 'Children are so flexible when they are born. They are also curious and moving all the time. Yoga allows them to focus and concentrate that energy. There are also some forms of yoga that help them express how they're feeling and help with communication. And for older children and teenagers, yoga can help with exam stress or any pressures they may be experiencing at school or in life elsewhere. Yoga teaches children to listen to their bodies and check in with themselves. It's empowering and, if taught properly, it can be fully inclusive. The other great thing about yoga is that it can be done at home in a small space, so it really is for everyone – even those who are unable to get to a class.'

Away from formal movement – even yoga – there are lots of types of movement that can simply be incorporated into everyday life: it's not glossy or sexy or glamorous, but simply walking more if you're able to, standing and stretching (whether you're an adult at your desk or a kid playing on the tablet while sitting on the sofa) or doing a ten-minute dance session on YouTube (before watching a YouTuber unbox ten Kinder eggs – what is this life?!) can be spontaneous, fun, practical, bonding and joyful. And it is all very, very valid.

These little moments are a great way to introduce some body appreciation into conversations with children too. Whether it's about appreciating how our legs carry us up a big hill, or how our arms can reach up really high when we stretch, or how our shoulders are great at moving to a beat, moments of movement are a fantastic opportunity to start introducing an awareness of all the ways our bodies show up for us every single day.

A note on privilege

I couldn't let this chapter pass without another note on privilege. Not a day goes by without parents being bombarded with information about the importance of exercise, and I think it's misguided to assume that anyone not taking part in movement is doing so simply because they can't be bothered.

Jake Gifford, MSc, is a PhD researcher and personal trainer who runs the platform @thephitcoach. 'The latest figures from Sport England identify children in the lowest income bracket as reporting the lowest activity levels, while children in the highest income bracket are reporting the highest levels,' says Jake.[17] 'This isn't a reflection of moral virtue across the social classes, rather how structural barriers, such as income, impact how children may or may not be able to be active.'

It's not just about income though, as Jake explains: 'It's also about other social factors – such as housing, neighbourhood safety, access to green space and leisure facilities – which can sometimes determine whether it's feasible or safe for children to engage with movement and whether parents are able to support them while juggling other challenges. If we don't consider factors such as these, there's a real possibility that policies and interventions aimed at children are likely to leave the most disadvantaged behind – evidence has already emerged showing this to be the case.'[18]

In 2019 I was invited on to a radio show to talk about a new report warning that children were too sedentary. The host asked me how much exercise my kids got and I told him that, depending on the day, it could be between one or two hours. He seemed impressed, but I then stressed that there are multiple reasons for this: we live in a village within walking distance of our school, so we walk there every day. We also have a park nearby with good-quality play equipment, and we live in the countryside with lots of access to safe wide-open spaces.

My children go to a school which offers extracurricular sporting opportunities, and I am able to pay for them to attend swimming, gymnastics and dance lessons. Plus, they currently enjoy these things, so there is no conflict or persuasion required to get them there. I am fully aware my circumstances are not the same for everyone, and I think it is hugely important that any conversation around kids' movement needs to recognise that not all children are on an equal playing field (pun intended).

As a society, if we care about children moving more then we not only need to take the diet culture out of movement but we also need to create safe, accessible, inclusive spaces for them to engage in exercise. There needs to be investment in play equipment, sports education and fun movement opportunities for *all* children, not just the nondisabled and smaller bodied ones who live in areas with access to safe play spaces and parents who have the time and resources to take them to these spaces.

BODY HAPPY KIDS TOOLKIT
Joyful Movement for Kids

The science

If you want to help your kids develop a positive relationship with movement for the rest of their life, then encouraging them to move for how it makes them feel (those 'intrinsic motivators' we heard about on page 151) over how it makes them look (the 'extrinsic motivators') is key.

We've also heard that function-focused comments, as opposed to appearance-based ones, can improve mood and boost body appreciation, and that giving children access to a wide representation of diverse athletes will help them understand that movement is for everybody.

The thing about joyful movement is that it doesn't need to be planned – a spontaneous game of catch or a family hula-hooping competition (which I always lose at) can be just as beneficial as a family bike ride or a football lesson. Remember, all movement is valid.

With that in mind, don't see this planner as something you have to follow to the letter. Instead, use it as inspiration, a starter point, a source of ideas for ways to incorporate movement into the life of the children in your care in an inclusive, happy and joyful way. You never know, you might find it useful for yourself too!

The tool: a joyful movement planner

	ACTIVITY	TIP
Monday	Kitchen disco	Movement can be spontaneous, fun and silly. It doesn't have to be an elaborate activity that's been planned out for hours beforehand. Kitchen (or any room for that matter) discos count too! For older kids and teens, this could be a fun time to learn some TikTok dances together. (For TikTok novices, open the app, go to the 'discover' page and search 'dance with TikTok'. And if you want more dance moves you can copy, you'll find lots of other great free resources online away from TikTok (see Resources, page 233).

	ACTIVITY	TIP
Tuesday	Organised sport (football, swimming, netball, martial arts, tennis, gymnastics – anything goes!)	Organised sport can be a great way to build social connections for kids, as well as foster discipline, boost self-esteem and give children the chance to experience failure (losing) in a safe and supporting setting. It's about more than just moving their bodies, but nevertheless sports also come with all the other intrinsic benefits of movement too.
Wednesday	Yoga	There are some great free yoga sessions for kids online (see Resources, page 233).
Thursday	Trip to the park	Don't overthink it. Even half an hour running off steam at the park counts as movement.
Friday	Family bubble party	Celebrate the end of the week with a family bubble party. Blow the bubbles and jump, hop and reach to pop them. There are lots of eco-friendly bubble mixture recipes online if you want to make your own.
Saturday	Running	If team sports aren't something your kids enjoy then they might be interested in running. There are running events for kids across the country (see Resources, page 233), or you could just organise a family run round the local park.

	ACTIVITY	TIP
Sunday	Family movement (a bike ride, scooter trip or a walk)	Avoid framing the activity as 'exercise'. Instead talk about the fun adventure, a chance to get outside in nature, as well as how the activity will boost 'happy hormones' (endorphins) and help build stamina and strength.

Extra tips

Being everyday active: Incorporating movement as just part of day-to-day activities is a great way to get kids moving – it doesn't always have to be an 'activity'. Don't underestimate the little things, if you're able to do them. Walking to school, for example, or taking the stairs over the lift, or just doing some simple stretches with the kids when you wake up (if you have time – I know how hectic mornings with children can be!) are all valid.

Representation matters: Introduce the children in your care to a wide range of athletes to show them that movement is for every body. Here's a list of inspiring sporting heroes to get you started:

- » Prince Fielder
- » Jessamyn Stanley
- » Louise Green
- » Scott Reardon
- » Leah Gilbert
- » Peter Crouch
- » Sarah Robles
- » Marcel Hug

- » Krista Henderson
- » Mirna Valerio
- » Valerie Sagun
- » Dana Falsetti
- » Jill Angie
- » Vince Wilfork
- » Schuyler Bailar

CHAPTER 7

'Social Media is Bad for Body Image', and Other Myths

Social media gets a bad rap, but this chapter is here to show that, when it comes to body image, the reality is far from clear-cut. From #fitspo to #BoPo, social media can be as problematic as it can be supportive, a tool for fuelling body hate as much as for fuelling body love.

In this chapter we're going to hear from people using social media in a positive way and will get their tips for raising kids who don't fall down the rabbit hole of comparison. Plus, we'll learn about some of the research into body image and social media, and will discover how this might inform our choices as adults in helping the children in our care have a happy relationship with their social apps.

At the end of this chapter you'll find an evidence-based toolkit to help your family navigate the sometimes murky world of social media to get the best out of it when it comes to body image (page 180).

A PICTURE PAINTS A THOUSAND WORDS

The picture caught my eye. On the left, a woman in mismatched underwear, unbrushed hair, shoulders slumped. Dark circles framed her unsmiling eyes. I saw myself in her. But on the right – hope! – the same woman transformed into sleek matching underwear, shoulders back, hands on hips, a wide grin plastered on her beaming face. The words underneath the photo: 'HOW I LOST THE BABY WEIGHT!'

The video began with the same woman covering her face with her hands, laughing, admitting she was *so embarrassed* for us all to see her 'before photo'. She then launched into a snappy 15-minute video about how she had lost the weight. It seemed so easy. I was rapt and, judging from the amount of views and likes the video had got, so was everyone else.

I left YouTube and found the woman on Instagram. There she was, #LivingHerBestLife, laughing and carefree, swishing her perfect hair, flashing her perfectly toned tummy on a white-sand beach surrounded by beautiful children. If I could just make myself look like her 'after photo', maybe I'd get a piece of that sunshine life too.

And as I took note of her 'morning routine' and jotted down 'what she ate in a day', carefully planning my own 'easy mum workout routine', I failed to recognise the alarmingly obvious: if I, as a 30-year-old woman, could get so sucked into believing the Insta-hype, what hope did children have?

Ironically, it was social media that fuelled my body shame, but it was also social media that saved me. A year later I discovered another woman laughing and carefree on a beach, except this woman didn't have a toned stomach. She showed me I could wear a bikini on a beach and #LiveMyBestLife without having abs of steel or a thigh gap. As I scrolled through her feed I saw lots of pictures of her enjoying life in the body she had without sharing tips for trying to change it, and as I clicked through the hashtags on her captions I found others doing the same. In this alternative Instagram universe people didn't measure everything they ate, or share 'body-sculpting work-outs', or wear torn and old mismatched underwear until their bodies were small enough to be rewarded with something more glamorous.

We can scoff at Instagram or TikTok or YouTube (or what-ever app is in vogue at the time you're reading this), but as of July 2020, 4.7 billion people were using social media – that's around half the world's population.[1] And in the second it just took you to read that sentence, at least 12 new people some-where in the world will have signed up. Social media massively influences us, from who we vote for to what we eat for dinner, and surveys estimate around 90 per cent of teenagers are on social networking sites.[2] Social media is not going anywhere anytime soon.

The positive of this is that there are many good sides to social media, and if it can influence mainstream society in a negative way, it also has the power to influence our collect-ive public consciousness in a positive way. From TV shows to books to changes in the law via lobbying and campaigns, social media can be a force for change. In fact, without social media this very book would likely not exist.

Maybe the issue isn't social media itself then, but rather what we do when we're on there. There's some research to show that following people online who talk negatively about their bodies and being exposed to body-shaming talk from others can make us feel worse about our own bodies.[3] Meanwhile, there's also evidence that following accounts with body-positive content can boost body image.[4]

Blaming social media for our kids feeling bad about their bodies both takes the power away from us as adults to do anything to help and removes the responsibility.

SNAPCHAT DYSMORPHIA AND THE RISE OF FACE FILTER CULTURE

In 2018 a new phenomenon hit the headlines: 'Snapchat dysmorphia'. Coined in a paper published in the *JAMA Facial Plastic Surgery* journal, scientists warned of a new mental illness primarily affecting teenagers wanting plastic surgery to look like their filtered selfies.[5]

Plastic surgeons shared stories of patients ditching the celebrity inspiration in favour of photos of their own filtered faces, as apps dedicated to simple 'tweaks' make filtered faces the norm. With a few quick taps you can smooth skin, widen eyes, whiten teeth, slim down or enhance curves. Sometimes these filters are so subtle it's not clear they're even there, and it's not just limited to Instagram or Snapchat. If you've had to do any video calls recently you may have noticed that online services such as Zoom even carry a beautifying filter.

There is no doubt that being constantly exposed to these types of images can wreak havoc on the way we view ourselves. Teens are no longer just comparing themselves to the airbrushed images of celebrities in magazines, they're now comparing themselves to their best mate's edited selfies too. Sure, Kim Kardashian has a whole glam squad at her disposal, but if the person you're comparing yourself to has a life very like yours, it might be harder to justify why you can't look as polished as they do.

COMPARISON IS THE THIEF OF JOY

If you think this just affects teenagers, think again. Dr Amy Slater is associate professor and co-director at the Centre for Appearance Research at the University of the West of England. Much of her research is into body image and children, as well as the impact of social media on body image. 'There are lots of websites now which are full of appearance-focused games for children,' says Amy. 'While a lot of these games are dress-up games, some of the ones I've researched are even more concerning in that they are focused on changing appearance – and these are aimed at girls between six and nine years old. There are cosmetic surgery games and apps in which young people are told how easy and important it is to change their appearance to suit a societal ideal. One experimental study I did with eight- and nine-year-old girls in the UK found that the girls who played the appearance-focused game desired a thinner body and had a stronger preference for traditionally feminine careers. We also found that in only ten minutes of game play we can see an immediate negative impact on young children. If this is the result after just ten minutes, what's the cumulative effect over a lifetime?'

Many online games and apps aimed at kids act as an introduction to social media, so although very young children may not be scrolling through Instagram or sharing images on Snapchat, if they have access to the Internet then it's likely they aren't immune to the effect of social media.

COMMUNITY

This is the good news bit. Social media is more than just selfies. It's also a place to find community and solidarity in shared experience. For children who may not feel like they belong in their real-life communities, their online world can become even more important.

In 2012 Common Sense Media found that teenagers were more likely to report that social media had a positive impact on their social and emotional lives than a negative one.[6] We shouldn't underestimate the importance of this, particularly when it comes to health.

In his book *Together*, Dr Vivek Murthy warns: 'People with strong social relationships are 50 percent less likely to die prematurely than people with weak social relationships. Even more striking, the impact of lacking social connection on reducing lifespan is equal to the risk of smoking fifteen cigarettes a day, and it's greater than the risk associated with obesity, excess alcohol consumption and lack of exercise. Simply put . . . weak social connections can be a significant danger to our health.'[7]

Social media can provide that connection in a way that many spaces in real life don't. As parents, it can be scary to think of our kids being part of a community that we're not involved in, but Becky Young and Harri Rose, who run the platform Anti Diet Riot Club, say it's not something to fear: 'This feeling of belonging is really important,' says Harri, who is also the author of *You Are Enough*.[8] 'Validation is what children and adults really need to thrive in this world, and that ultimately is the biggest power of social media.'

Anti Diet Riot Club is a 'rebel community fighting diet culture' with a vibrant online space, as well as real-life workshops, festivals and life-drawing classes. There's even a travelling tour bus, and many of the people who participate in the community find them online first. 'Although social media is increasingly saturated by people trying to sell you things, at the same time, people's profiles are not explicitly from the outset controlled by corporations or advertisers or other things that mainstream media is,' says Becky. 'So there is a lot more room to have ugly conversations, talk about things that are a bit messier, and represent a more diverse experience that mainstream media don't want to cover.'

Having open conversations and shared connections is important no matter the subject matter, but when it comes to issues that may go against the mainstream narrative, having a community to support you is vital.

'One of the first steps in trying to engage with your body differently is to opt out of diet culture and, where possible, all of the other power structures around it, and for that you need to find a community. It makes it so much easier if you have people around you, whether in real life or online, who can help you grow,' says Becky.

'I grew up in a really small village in west Wales and I just think about all the teenagers who are living in isolated areas not able to see people who look like them, or not having shared experiences. That to me is the absolute beauty and power of having a community online,' agrees Harri.

The community aspect of social media also empowers young people in ways they might not be able to experience in real life, as they can use their likes as a form of currency, spending them on the things they think matter. This can go both ways, of course, as there's a danger of those very likes becoming a measure of self-worth. But I think it's important to acknowledge that, for many teenagers, having the power to engage and take part in conversations can bring huge rewards, particularly if the conversations are about enacting social change.

IDENTITY

Being a teenager can be hard, exciting and confusing. It's a time when you're working out who you are and what you believe in, as well as trying to fit into a world that isn't always accepting of the person you're becoming. I often feel relieved that I got to do this in the nineties, away from the glare of a social media spotlight; exploring my identity as an adult online has proved hard enough without the confusing body changes and friendship dramas I experienced as a teen.

In fact, the famous psychologist Erik Erikson said 'identity exploration' is the key 'work' of adolescence.[9] He believed that teenagers who get to explore their independence and develop a sense of self with proper encouragement and reinforcement will grow up with a strong sense of who they are, feeling in control and independent. When it comes to body image, this means multiple things. Teenagers' bodies are changing, but so is the way they link their identity and self-worth to the body they live in. The social pressure to look a certain way and present their identity and values through their appearance ramps up a notch, and social media can amplify this all even more.

This isn't always a negative thing though. While social media can be a very public way to do the work of identity development, it can also give young people a safe space to explore their values, beliefs and the things that make them who they are. Not all teenagers want to dive headfirst into books. This is where social media can be a powerful tool for identity exploration, giving them a place to discover new ideas and conversations to help their growth, including introducing them to the books and films that might help them learn about a subject in more detail.

Kenny Ethan Jones is a model and activist who made history fronting a period campaign. He explains how social media has given him a space to tell his story on his own terms, which has helped shape the adult he is today: 'I've had an Instagram account since 2012 but at that time it was just for myself, it wasn't to serve as activism. But in a way, even when I was just on Myspace, just my existence on the Internet was activism because I've always been open about being trans.'

For Kenny, Instagram gave him not only a place to share his own story but an opportunity to learn more about himself by reading about the experiences of other people too. 'Around the time the period campaign launched I started to get a surge in following – I'd never been in a position where I had that many eyes on me and I had to make a decision on what I would use my platform for, and what it would become. In terms of the personal perspective, I started to educate myself on other people's voices too. And I started to realise what privilege was because I hadn't really understood that as a concept before. I started to learn how my race – being a mixed-race man – played into that. Instagram gave me a space to connect different pockets of knowledge and eventually it came to make sense and made me the person I am today.

'When I started to talk more about periods and then conversations came down to biological sex, that's when people started to argue against my existence, because they said you can't say you're a man if you own a vagina,' explains Kenny. 'At that time I had to build tough skin. I decided to know that what they were saying wasn't true and be confident with who I am. Around this time I also started finding the body-positive community and seeing all these wonderful different body types. I had never really embraced the variety of bodies there were before, and I started to realise that I didn't necessarily have the greatest relationship with my body. I wouldn't say it was negative, but it wasn't pure; it wasn't me looking inwards. It was society projecting what I thought my body should look like. I've always felt like I spent my adult years unlearning what I learned as a child, and the way I felt about my body was one of those things. Finding that space online made me realise every-one was accepted, regardless of shape, ability, whatever. We are all just humans and everybody deserves love and respect'.

Kenny's empowering experience of social media is, he says, largely down to the fact that he's in charge of his own narra-tive, which isn't the case with other forms of media. 'People who work in corporations or at big magazines are often white, cisgendered, privileged people, but social media gives power to people to voice their own stories. Although mainstream media sometimes makes way for people like myself, they still get to tell my story how they want to. So the power isn't with me anymore, it's with them and how they decide to project it.

Social media gives me the ability to take control of what I'm saying and not allow anyone else to shape that into a way that suits the bigger media.'

REPRESENTATION

This word comes up time and time again when we talk about body image and, unsurprisingly, it's a huge part of why social media can be a source of comfort for how children feel about their bodies. Not only can social media provide a place for kids to see a broader range of bodies than they might do in mainstream media, but this representation on social media can also filter through to mainstream media.

Although big brands are often criticised for co-opting body positivity (and I'd obviously never support a diet brand using this movement to sell their products), the fact that TV and billboard ads are now regularly incorporating a wider range of people with a broader range of bodies in their ad campaigns is, I think, a good thing. This doesn't mean we don't still have a long way to go, but it's a step in a more positive direction from the nineties that I grew up in.

The 'This Girl Can' campaign is a great example of how social media can be a force for good in the realm of representation. In 2014, 1.75 million fewer women were exercising regularly than men.[10] Sport England set out to close this gap with their innovative campaign to remove the most powerful barrier stopping women from getting active: the fear of judgement. By creating a campaign celebrating women of all shapes, sizes and abilities enjoying movement, Sport England encouraged 2.9 million women aged 14–60 to get active. Representation matters.

Stevie Blaine is an LGBTQIA+ and body acceptance activist. He agrees that representation is one of the reasons social media can be such a powerful tool when it comes to feeling better about your body. In fact, it's one of the main reasons he set up his @bopo.boy platform – to provide representation for the many men and boys struggling with body image.

'Originally, Instagram was the tool I used to self-deprecate,' explains Stevie. 'It was the place I went to follow all these fitness models and hyper-masculine men. I thought I'd be able to look like them if I worked hard enough – their posts would spur me on to the next diet or push me into the next exercise regime. It was the tool I used to break down my relationship with my body, and because these were the accounts I followed I thought this was how everyone must look.'

Stevie says his experience was not unusual, and it wasn't until he started sharing his authentic story and struggles with body image that he realised how many other men and boys were battling body insecurities too. 'Within men there's this toxic masculinity to always be inside this "man box", thinking we need to be strong and never talk about our emotions, as well as look physically strong. And nowadays, when it comes to grooming and aesthetics, men are under pressure as well as women. If you look at the major cosmetics brands, they all have lines for men. On shows like *Love Island*, the guys on there all put a huge amount of work into their appearance – going to the gym every day and tanning, getting their teeth done and getting their eyebrows done. The men who follow my account tell me I've allowed them this space to talk about things they may not even feel comfortable talking about with their own wife or girlfriend, because society puts that pressure on them to be strong.'

The bodies we most commonly see in mainstream media don't reflect the diversity of real life, so we can then assume that thin, toned, sculpted bodies are 'the norm' and feel wrong if we don't look like that. If this is then what we see all over social media too it can exacerbate that feeling. Stevie's turning point came when he stopped comparing his body to the fitness models he'd been following and started filling his feed with a much broader representation of different types of bodies. 'Social media is now a never-ending tool of love and support, where I only see bodies that are diverse. I've built and sculpted this perfect community of pure representation. Social media is the one place you have a bit of control over and the ability to see what you want. Once I used social media to unfollow the accounts making me feel bad and follow a plethora of accounts to see a whole range of different people with different bodies, I felt better. I could see the beauty in them, so I could see the beauty in me too. I realised it's the differences that make us all unique and incredible.'

Stevie's experience is reflected in the research. A 2019 study found that women can build positive body image by controlling what they see on social media.[11] The researchers (which included Dr Amy Slater, who we heard from earlier on) discovered that unfollowing or blocking idealised accounts, and following more body-positive accounts, could create a social media environment that could help people feel better – instead of worse – about their bodies.

It's not just about following body-positive accounts though. Widening the type of content we see online to include all the things we're interested in – not just bodies (top tip: #DogsofInstagram is your friend) – and sometimes following people with a different perspective to our own can be another important step in using social media in a positive way. This can reduce our chances of living in 'filter bubbles' or echo chambers, where we only ever see one type of opinion or style of content. In an age where society is arguably more divided than ever, this could turn social media into a unifying force rather than a tool for division.

Hopefully by now you can see that social media doesn't have to be the catalyst for body shame that you might have previously thought it to be. And with this next toolkit you'll be able to ramp up the benefits for the kids in your care too.

BODY HAPPY KIDS TOOLKIT

How to Use Social Media Responsibly and Positively

The science

Psychologists say the best way to teach children healthy habits is to role model them. This isn't just about getting our kids to use social media in a positive way – we need to look at the way we use it too. If you find you feel worse about your body after a quick scroll on your socials, then now might be the time to make some changes. Trust me, it's liberating.

This isn't some wishy-washy advice – the research backs it up. Researchers in Israel found that the more time girls spent on

Facebook, the more they suffered conditions of eating disorders, poor body image and a negative approach to eating.[12] It's not all scary reading though, because the girls whose parents were involved in their media usage fared much better. When parents knew what their daughters were viewing online and talked to them about what they saw, the girls were more empowered and resilient to some of the negative messages.

This might sound straightforward, but the fact that social media now lives in our pocket 24/7, just a swipe away, can make it a tough thing to monitor. In fact, this easy access is part of what makes social media so tempting – another part is the effect it has on the brain. A study from Harvard University found that posting something online lights up the same part of the brain that ignites when taking an addictive substance.[13] It's no wonder we're all on our phones more than ever.

We can't get rid of social media though, and the best way to help our kids use it responsibly and positively is to look at how we use it ourselves, as well as giving plenty of safe opportunities for the children in our care to talk to us about what they see when they're on there. This is where this tool comes in.

The tool: a family social media agreement

The key word in this tool is 'agreement'. Instead of seeing this as a list of rules, look at it as a starting point for a *negotiation* with your family for how you all agree to use social media. You can use this as a place to hold each other accountable (and it goes both ways – kids keeping adults accountable too!).

> » Our family phone-free hour is: _____. During
>   this time we agree to turn off all phones and devices

and do something that makes ourselves and our bodies feel good instead. (Try some of the activities from the self-care starter kit in Chapter 3 – page 92 – or the joyful movement planner in Chapter 6 – page 162 – if you're in need of inspiration.)

» We agree not to have phones at the dinner table.

» On _____ every month we will have a 'social media blackout' day, where we agree not to use social media at all and to do something together instead.

» We agree to the following four-point plan when deciding to follow or engage with an account on social media:

1. Does this account make us feel good?
2. Is it diet culture in disguise? (Use the toolkit at the end of Chapter 2 to help you with this – page 60.)
3. Does this account share new ideas and experiences that inspire us and challenge us to think differently?
4. Does this account share pictures of bodies that look different from those we regularly see on TV and in magazines?

» We agree to discuss with each other what we see on social media, including if something has inspired or troubled us.

CHAPTER 8

Child's Play: The Impact of Toys on Kids' Body Image

How did we get to a place where children as young as three years old feel their bodies are wrong and kids as young as five say they need to go on a diet? I believe it's not one particular thing, but an amalgamation of many.

It's a sprinkling of 'childhood obesity' headlines, a pinch of social media filters and a dash of fatphobia in kids' cartoons. It's the Disney princesses and the way we talk to kids about health. But it's also the toys. And this is what we're going to explore here.

We'll look at how the toys in your kids' toy box might be contributing to a culture of body ideals, and what you can do to counteract some of the potential negativity. We'll get into it with the subject of gender stereotypes and get up close and personal with the likes of Barbie and Ken. And at the end of this chapter you'll find a toolkit that might come in handy the next time you're picking out a toy for the children in your life (page 195).

THE BEST OF INTENTIONS

Barbie was banned from our house. My mum talked about 'unrealistic bodies', but at the age of six I didn't really under-stand what that meant. Thirty years on I realise she was trying to protect me from some of the insidious messages coming my way about bodies and the role of women. It was a valiant effort and I applaud her for it. But still, I really wanted a Barbie.

When I first became a mum I vowed to ban Barbie too. My kids were only going to have wooden toys, or ones made from recycled materials, in gender-neutral colours. Ha ha ha. Their playroom is a treasure trove of sparkly princess outfits and Barbies nestled among train tracks, Sylvanian Families, Lego and pots of slime. I dream of a minimalist life, living on a yurt in the middle of a field, but somehow the sequin-encrusted plastic keeps coming into my house; the little combs, miniature high heels and teeny-weeny glittery miniskirts a reminder of everything I vowed my kids wouldn't have.

I live in a regular state of conflict between allowing my kids the freedom to play with the things that interest them and knowing the potential negative impact of some of the toys they love. What I have managed to do, though, is gain a sense of perspective. Just like I can't realistically stop them ever seeing a Disney film until there's a plus-size princess, I can't ban Barbie and her look-a-likes either.

Instead, I can make sure there are other types of toys on offer too, create a neutral approach to toys (I learned early on that trying to force some toys on to my kids had the opposite effect) and talk to my children about the fact that Barbie and Ken are a fantasy and that real human bodies rarely look like that. I hope this chapter will be a comforting read if, like me, you've struggled with this stuff too.

WHY TOYS MATTER

By now you're probably already aware of the impact of popular culture on body image. Although we haven't yet talked about TV and film (that's coming), it's safe to say popular culture plays a role in the way we think and feel about our bodies. The toys kids play with are the earliest form of popular culture they're exposed to. In fact, in a 2013 article in the *Independent* about the subject, toy expert Professor Jeffrey Goldstein told writers Jonathan Owen and Margi Murphy, 'Toys, and play in general, reflect what goes on around children.'[1] If you look at toys through the ages, it's an interesting reflection of what else is going on in the world. Don't believe me? Look at the hit toy of the seventies – the space hopper. This is essentially an exercise ball, which came out at precisely the time the fitness industry started booming.

The global toy market is estimated at over $90 billion, with the UK worth £3.2 billion alone.[2] Toys inspired by films and TV shows make up a huge proportion of that figure, and in 2016, two years after it was first released, toys based on the film *Frozen* helped toy company Hasbro top $5 billion revenue for the first time. YouTube is also big business in the toy market, with various YouTubers releasing their own toy lines. In 2018 Walmart announced a collaboration with the six-year-old star of *Ryan's World*, the biggest toy channel on

YouTube. Toys are not just linked to popular culture – they *are* popular culture.

If we can be aware of the impact of TV, film, magazines and social media on body image, then we need to understand that toys play a part too. What we see has a huge impact on how we view our bodies. But, more than that, the very nature of what we *do* with toys arguably gives them even more power when it comes to children's body image.

Toys are everywhere in childhood, and they form a vital part of how kids learn. Play is literally 'the work of childhood', according to the famous quote often attributed to psychologist Jean Piaget (although opinion is divided on this).[3] It's how children learn new skills, practise relationships, role-play different identities and make sense of the world. If the toys that children are playing with convey or reinforce certain messages about gender roles, bodies, health and beauty then this is something we need to be aware of. Like I said before, we can't just blame Instagram for bad body image.

Professor Christia Brown, author of *Parenting Beyond Pink & Blue*, explains that the toys we give our children matter more than we may realise.[4] 'Toys are how kids learn skills and traits; it's how they learn what's valued, and it's also how they learn what's expected. The toys we give them tell them what we value, what we want them to learn. So if we give them a science toy, for example, we're saying "we value this, we want you to learn this". Children learn something from every single toy they play with, not just the obviously educational ones, but we're not necessarily mindful of the things they're learning from every toy.'

Which takes us on to dolls, Barbie and the argument against Action Man …

THE LOWDOWN ON DOLLS

The messages children get from the toys they play with come at a time when they are still forming ideas about identity, the world and their place in it. Compare Action Man and Barbie, for example, and you'll see clear messages about gender roles – men are 'strong' and 'heroic' while women are fashion- and beauty-conscious. We'll delve deeper into this in a minute, but for now let's look at some of the ways kids could be learning about the 'perfect body' from the toys they're playing with.

In 1959 American toy manufacturer Mattel launched Barbie, a fashion doll. She was designed as an aspirational toy, with the creator, Ruth Handler (who named Barbie after her daughter, Barbara), explaining, 'My whole philosophy of Barbie was that, through the doll, the little girl could be anything she wanted to be. Barbie always represented the fact a woman has choices.'[5]

But with a body–fat ratio so low many researchers say she'd be unlikely to menstruate if she was a real-life human, Barbie's choices were arguably impacted by the way she looked. Through Barbie, little girls learned they could be an astronaut or a doctor, but only if they had white skin (the first Black Barbie wasn't launched until 1980), an impossibly tiny waist, long glossy hair and legs that went on for miles.

In her book *Body Wars*, Margo Maine, PhD, argues that if the original Barbie was a human, she'd be 5 feet 9 inches tall, with a 39-inch bust and an 18-inch waist, weighing no more than 110lb.[6] When researchers in South Australia scaled up Barbie to life-size proportions, they found the likelihood of a woman having her shape to be 1 in 100,000.[7] And if girls didn't get the thin memo then the 1965 Slumber Party Barbie certainly made it clear: she came complete with a set of scales permanently set to 110lb and a diet book telling her not to eat.

If this all sounds like a problem left in the sixties, think again. In 2006 researchers investigated whether playing with thin dolls affected the body image of girls aged five to eight years old.[8] The girls were divided into three groups and were given a Barbie, an Emme doll (US size 16) or no doll. And the results? Girls playing with Barbie reported 'lower body esteem and greater desire for a thinner body shape than girls in the other exposure conditions'.

Fast forward to today and Barbie's had a makeover. Along with the original thin Barbie, kids can now choose between 'curvy', 'tall' or 'petite' Barbie, and there are also versions of Barbie as a wheelchair user or with a prosthetic leg. This move in the direction of diversity is a good thing, particularly given that more than 100 Barbie dolls are sold every minute, so we can assume a lot of children own Barbies.[9] But how likely are kids to opt for the new range of Barbie when the original one still exists?

Not very likely, according to one study. In 2019 researchers asked a group of 84 girls aged three to ten years old to assign positive or negative traits to the four different types of Barbie.[10] Their results showed a clear preference to thin bodies among the children. What's more, the girls who reported feeling worse about their own body showed fewer negative attitudes towards the original (thin) Barbie. The internalised thin ideal runs deep, apparently.

And don't be fooled into thinking 'dolls' means I'm just talking about girls here. Let's assume you think Barbie is just for girls (which I don't, by the way), there's also research into the impact of action figures – or, as I like to call them, action *dolls* – on the body image of boys. (Notice how even the name is gendered – no 'dolls' for boys, despite it being the same type of toy.) While the original thin Barbie has an almost impossible figure, the same is true of G.I. Joe. Since it was launched in 1964, G.I. Joe's muscles got gradually bigger and more defined, with huge bulging biceps and an eight-pack. This is true of the new action dolls on the market today too, from the Marvel Legends dolls to the WWE dolls and all the superhero dolls around that are marketed at boys.

In a 2018 interview on CapeTalk radio Professor Kopano Ratele talked about this subject: 'The language that reinstates this two-sex model – this sexual dimorphism – is really important for a certain view about the world. The kind of bodies that the designers put on what is a male doll and a female doll, and right through the way toy shops are arranged, with the kind of toys that are "man toys" directed at male children, and then the toys directed at female children, leads to a certain view about gender. There's still a very powerful notion that masculinity is something that only is invested in male bodies. And so in the production of toys this view comes forth, because what we tend to see is the muscularity of these toys. In that moment something quite interesting – but also something that has serious social implications – happens. It says: "This is how men should look." It puts a particular kind of pressure on young men about the kind of work you have to do on the body.'[11]

Whether it's a thin doll with large breasts and a tiny waist or a muscly doll with an eight-pack and bulging biceps, the message is the same: this is the ideal body, and this is what we value. There's another element at play here too though, which leads us on to the argument for a gender-neutral approach to toys.

TOYS, GENDER STEREOTYPES AND BODY IMAGE

Go back to the dolls for a second and think about what they do, and how kids play with them. Action dolls which are typically marketed to boys have a range of movement and can bend and move in a variety of ways – they can stand and often hold things. As a result they can *do* things when they are played with – build castles, fight villains, drive trucks. Now think about the fashion dolls. These will often have no hinges on the joints, hands that can't hold things and tiny, angled feet – perfect for high heels but less great for standing. What can these dolls do? They can be dressed and have their hair brushed – no castle-building or villain-fighting for them!

It's not just the dolls though. Even brands like Lego have different ranges that are predicated on gender stereotypes. The fire engines, dumper trucks – and even the 'space exploration' sets – are in the 'City' range with blue packaging, marketed towards boys, while the ice skating rinks, tree houses and glamping sets, for example, are in their 'Friends' range with purple packaging, marketed towards girls. Interestingly, research into these different types of Lego sets suggests the colour and type of the toys doesn't just affect whether children choose to play with them – it impacts the very ways in which they play with them too.[12] Boys are encouraged to role-play skilled professions and be 'heroes', while girls are encouraged to focus on hobbies, being domestic and caring for others – as well as prioritising beauty.[13]

According to Professor Christia Brown, this is just one of the ways children learn about their roles in the world, and what their bodies are for, early on. 'If we had to boil it down to one

190

core difference, it's that we teach boys to do things and we teach girls to look a certain way. This plays out with body image, with appearance, with why girls are so highly sexualised, and the damage that comes with that and with how boys are taught to be active and agentic and strong.'

This might not seem like a big deal, but the repercussions are huge. 'With toys, children are playing the tasks of adulthood,' explains Christia. 'That's one reason I think gender stereotypes are so prevalent in toys, because we're training kids to diverge – often giving boys play tools and girls dolls. These toys tell children the ideal for what they are supposed to be like. Even Doctor Barbie has skinny jeans and highly sexualised clothes on under her lab coat, so it reinforces the idea that the feminine appearance is really important.'

This doesn't mean you need to necessarily go and bin all your Barbies. Instead, making sure children have a wide range of different types of toys might be the way forward. 'Fostering positive skills in human kids regardless of their gender is useful,' says Christia. 'For years there's been a consistent gender difference where boys have been better at spatial tasks. There are all these elaborate evolutionary and biological explanations as to why this may be the case, and why we have more men in engineering jobs for example. But a team of researchers who were trying to teach children better spatial skills (and weren't about gender at all) gave kids things like Lego to play with, and found that after a week of doing these little spatial tasks the gender differences in elementary school kids were completely erased.[14] So if you'd given girls Lego all along then we wouldn't need an evolutionary explanation at all! Historically, we've had such gender segregation we've developed really different skill sets because they've been encouraged from early on. Women often grow up way more comfortable with babies, for example, but it's largely because in childhood we were given a baby doll to care for and a pretend diaper to change. I think we short-change boys by not giving them those opportunities because they are good skills to have. Doll play can teach a lot of good stuff, but it's stuff we should all be learning, not just half the population.'

But what does this have to do with the way kids feel about their bodies, I hear you cry! Well, quite a lot actually. By raising girls to think their sole purpose is to be pretty and *be*, and raising boys to think their sole purpose is to be strong and *do*, we are placing a huge burden on their shoulders and potentially setting them up to feel like their bodies never match up to how they understand 'pretty' or 'strong' should look. It's also perpetuating a really narrow view of gender, and automatically excludes any child who doesn't fit these gender role expectations, as well as excluding any gender non-conforming child who doesn't identify with the gender they were assigned at birth. Gender stereotypes in toys, then, can potentially impact the way children of *all* genders feel about their bodies.

THE GOOD (TOY) NEWS

The thought of binning all my kids' Barbies and getting rid of all their Disney Princess dolls fills me with dread – I simply can't handle the tears. So instead I talk to my daughters about the fact that real humans don't often have bodies like their Barbies. This is a tool known as 'media literacy', and we'll meet it in the next chapter (page 207) as a useful trick to have up your sleeve when talking to children about something they see on the TV, in a film, on YouTube, in a magazine – or even on social media. It gives them the ability to unpick the message so they are more resilient against it, and it works with toys too. Experts say that, although the toys kids play with do matter, what matters more is the influence of the adults in a child's life when it comes to body image and self-esteem, so don't underestimate the power you play in that (even if your child has a toy box full of Barbies or action dolls).

Another way you can counteract some of the negativity is allowing your kids the opportunity to play with a wide range of toys. Toy swapping with other families is a great way to broaden your kids' toy horizons – if they have children who are a different gender to yours, then all the better. And some areas have toy libraries, where you can borrow a range of toys too.

While the toy industry might have been part of the problem when it comes to bad body image in kids, it's also proving to be part of the solution too. There are now various ranges of dolls that are designed to challenge gender stereotypes and unrealistic body ideals. And although the research shows that kids still favour the thin, original Barbie over the other types in the Fashionista range Mattel launched in 2016, the fact we even have a wider range of Barbies to choose from is proof of consumer power. There are also lots of toy brands now shunning the traditional gender-stereotyped marketing and positioning themselves as 'gender-neutral', and the campaign Let Toys Be Toys – which grew out of a thread on parenting site Mumsnet – has led to many retailers removing 'girls' and 'boys' signage in their stores.

This is proof that collectively we can make a difference to the play opportunities afforded to our kids and hopefully pave the way for future generations to grow up surrounded by fewer

narrow gender stereotypes that can impact how they feel about their bodies (and themselves).

We are not passive and powerless to do anything in the face of this stuff. We can be part of the problem, perpetuating gender stereotypes and narrow body ideals in the toys we allow our kids to play with. But we can also be part of the solution too.

BODY HAPPY KIDS TOOLKIT

How to Encourage Positive Body Image through Toys

The science

This toolkit is based on everything we've learned in this chapter about gender stereotypes and the impact of body ideals in toys. We know that playing with thin dolls can affect girls' body image and we know that playing with muscly dolls can make boys feel bad about their bodies too. But we also know that giving children equal opportunities to play with a wide range of toys can eliminate the 'gender segregation' we heard about earlier.

This tool can be used alongside the one in the next chapter to help build resilience to some of the messages which might make the kids in your care question their bodies, as well as giving them the tools to call out these messages in the first place.

The tool: the toy test

Follow these questions to help decide if a toy is going to make it into your kids' toy box:

1. Is the toy marketed specifically towards a particular gender?

Talk to your child about how all toys are for all children. Remove the packaging. If you can, introduce a wide range of different types of toys (e.g. dolls, trucks, animals and building blocks). You could use a toy library to find a range of different toys without having to purchase new ones.

We're all good!

2. If the toy is a doll, does it have an unrealistic body shape for a real person?

Talk to your child about how all bodies are good bodies. Introduce diversity through books and other toys. Use the other tools throughout the book to continue to promote body respect, diversity and acceptance, to build resilience against the message this toy may be sending.

Yay! Share your find on social media so we can all get one too and congratulate the brand on a job well done!

3. Is the toy promoting the idea that to be happy, popular or successful you should look a certain way?

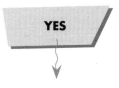

Show your child a diverse range of images of successful, happy and popular people who don't fit the narrow, idealised norm of what we're told is the 'perfect' body. You can use the suggestions in the toolkit at the end of Chapter 6 for this (page 165).

We love this toy.

4. Is the toy part of a wider range that shows a diverse variation of bodies and people?

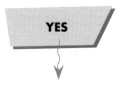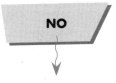

Hurrah! Share the love on social media and let us all know about it.

There are a variety of dolls now that represent a more diverse range of people with different types of bodies. If your child is wedded to Barbie you might like to consider one of the newer models instead of the original. And you can mix these up with other types of toys too.

CHAPTER 9

Bodies on Screen

Television gets the blame for a lot of our body image blues, but is it something we even need to worry about until our kids are old enough to watch *Love Island*? The truth is that the messages coming at children making them question their bodies are rife, way before they're teenagers and into reality TV.

From Disney to *Peppa Pig*, their favourite YouTubers and even the educational shows on telly, diet culture can seep out of the soft glow of the screen worshipped at the centre of our living rooms right from the toddler years.

In this chapter we'll explore where some of these messages come from and what you can do to stop them landing quite so hard. Don't worry, you don't need to ditch Disney. Instead, we'll look at ways to pinpoint the negative messages and then counteract them.

WHEN TV GETS TOXIC

It's late on a winter's night in 2014 and I am lapping up my latest TV obsession: *Pretty Little Liars*, a show about a group of popular, thin, stylish teenage girls navigating the mysterious disappearance of a friend.

With exhaustion at an all-time high and confidence at an all-time low, it provides just the right hit of escapism I'm seeking without requiring any brain power severely drained by my sleep-phobic second daughter, born a couple of months earlier. I devour each episode with the same enthusiasm my newborn latches to my nipple, completely unaware of the impact the show is having on my already fragile body image.

By day I'm hit by social media ads telling me how to 'lose the post-baby belly fat fast' and by night I'm soaking up every word of a TV show where one of the main characters lives in fear of returning to her 'before' body. There's a line in an episode I'll never forget, because it made me conscious of a part of my body I'd never really thought about before. A 'mean girl' is told smugly, 'That dress gives you back fat.' It's not her bullying behaviour that's the subject of the taunt, but her body. I stopped watching the show not long after that.

What we watch matters, and a famous study in Fiji in the nineties proved this to be the case.[1] In 1995 a team of researchers investigated the impact of TV on a group of teenage girls on the island. Traditionally, the Fijian body ideal was robust and rounded; 'You've gained weight' was a compliment and dieting was actively discouraged. Eating disorders in Fiji were virtually unheard of, but just three years after TV arrived, everything changed. In 1995, when TV had only just landed, the researchers surveyed a group of girls and found almost none reported feeling 'too big' or were tempted to diet. By 1998, just three years after shows like *Beverly Hills, 90210* and *Melrose Place* started to be beamed in by satellite, the numbers had shot up. By this time 69 per cent of the girls reported dieting and 74 per cent reported feeling 'too big'.

That was in the nineties, but the impact of TV on body image is now arguably stronger than ever. In 2019 the Mental Health Foundation released a report in the UK showing that 24 per cent of 18–24-year-olds find reality TV shows like *Love Island* make them feel bad about their bodies.[2] And in January of 2020 UK Anti-Doping was so concerned about the impact of the new winter series of *Love Island* they issued a warning on the use of steroids for young men tempted to self-medicate their way to the ripped, sculpted look so popular with the show's contestants.[3]

Shows like *Love Island*, *Beverly Hills, 90210* and *Pretty Little Liars* are one thing, but if you think the ideal body messages start here, think again.

DADDY PIG, DISNEY AND FATPHOBIA IN KIDS' TV

What was your favourite Disney film when you were little? Mine was *The Little Mermaid*, a film about a thin, white, wide-eyed princess mermaid being tricked by an evil, greedy, jealous fat octopus. Watching that film now as an adult, I can see that Ursula is the most badass of baddies, and her complete owner-ship of her body and non-apologetic taking up of space is very cool. But as a kid, I wasn't able to do a feminist reading of the film or see her as an icon of female empowerment. All I saw was a character whose body was used to signify greed, a rampant ego and dishonesty, and who ultimately met a sticky end when the heroic prince literally rammed his massive boat into her, piercing her heart and getting rid of her for good. The message couldn't have been more simple: thin = good and fat = bad (and, by the way, beware if you're fat because the patriarchy will come for you and pierce you through the heart).

Throughout the ages we've had many Disney baddies, some big, some small, some tall, some short. And we've had many Disney princesses, but we've never had a fat one. It's almost as if centring a character with a bigger body as the main protagonist, not the villain or the jolly best friend, is the last taboo. As a child growing up watching Disney movies, it seemed clear that to get love, be successful or be at the centre of the story, you needed to look a certain way – and being thin was top of the list.

It's not just Disney. Anyone who's ever seen *Peppa Pig* – a cartoon that's now been translated into over 40 languages and gained millions of fans worldwide – will be familiar with how Daddy Pig's belly is often the punchline of the joke. In fact, a 2017 study found that 84 per cent of kids' movies and shows include weight-based stigma and insults about body size, often showing up multiple times throughout a movie.[4] And in 2014 a study found that 58.3 per cent of kids' TV shows contain negative comments related to the characters' weight or appearance.[5]

Victoria Welsby is the creator of Fierce Fatty Academy, a fat-positive body acceptance coach and a TEDx speaker. 'Studies have shown that kids from a very young age begin to understand, through the people they're interacting with and the media they're consuming, who the correct people, the right people, the safe people are – which is often straight-sized white people,' explains Victoria. 'And if you're not introducing a variety of bodies into children's lives they will pick up the message that fat bodies, brown bodies and disabled bodies are not as good as thin, white, nondisabled bodies.'

This lack of diversity can have a huge impact, says Victoria. 'I personally remember this because I can't think of any fat representation that was positive. It was all negative. I loved Roald Dahl's books and Disney, but all the fat characters were the lazy, slovenly ones, or the funny one, or the matriarch. They were never the protagonist, never the hero. They were just there to continue the stereotype that we have about fat people. This directly affected me. I remember when I was about five years old and it was a hot summer's day at school and at the time it was cool to tie your shirt into a little knot to show your stomach – but I knew that I wasn't allowed to do that with my body because I had a little tummy. I had learned my body was bad. No one had come up to me and said, "Victoria your body is bad", but I'd learned through osmosis.'

One way you can counteract these negative messages is to actively seek out positive representation elsewhere (hot tip: go to Instagram right now and look up the account @neoqlassicalart). Plus equipping your kids with some basic media literacy skills will prove invaluable too – the toolkit at the end of this chapter will help with that (page 207).

WHAT ABOUT YOUTUBE?

YouTube sits in the hazy realm between TV and social media. I've decided to include it in this chapter because the platform now creates its own TV shows and films, and with the arrival of Internet TV many kids now watch YouTube on telly like a regular channel.

A study by the UK media regulator Ofcom found that 80 per cent of children use YouTube, with nearly half of eight- to eleven-year-olds choosing YouTube over other subscription on-demand services like Netflix and Amazon Prime.[6] But YouTube differs to regular TV channels like the BBC and ITV because, at the time of writing, it's not regulated in the same way (although the introduction of Ofcom as a new Internet regulator – announced in 2020 – will go some way to changing that).

On YouTube children can find clips of their favourite TV shows, as well as videos created by their favourite vloggers, who they will often view in the same way as a friend or older sibling. In a report by Revealing Reality commissioned by Ofcom, 40 kids were surveyed.[7] One of the responses they shared came from 'Meredith, aged 16', who said she liked watching a certain fitness vlogger because she is a 'source of advice'. I looked up this particular vlogger and found a wealth of videos about calorie counting and getting 'shreddy'. These videos aren't protected by a content warning or a watershed, and they can be viewed by anyone with access to YouTube. But add to this the fact that many thousands of kids hang on the words of this vlogger and many others like her, and that their marker of trust comes from how many followers she has rather than any professional qualification in nutrition or dietetics, and things get worrying.

Remember back in Chapter 7 we heard from Dr Amy Slater (page 171)? She talked about the impact of appearance-based online games on kids' body image. Her advice about navigating these games stands for other types of media too, including YouTube. 'It's important to be mindful of the messages that might be coming from particular platforms,' says Amy. 'So, for younger children, to think about what messages they're getting from whatever form of entertainment they're consuming and what effect this has over time. And to ask how all of these messages sit within this cultural landscape that is constantly telling us that the most important thing we should value about ourselves and others is how we look on the outside and what we can do to improve that.'

Amy recommends building media literacy skills (which we'll get to in a second), and part of this is about teaching kids to determine where they're getting their information from, which includes recognising whether something is an #ad or #spon. 'We used to only have the option to watch a television programme with discrete blocks of advertising,' says Amy. 'But social media and YouTube have blurred the boundaries of advertising. When we have the concept of celebrities and influencers it's sometimes difficult to tell what is an ad and what is not.'

This is an important point when it comes to YouTube because kids might be watching their favourite vlogger, who they trust and admire, and unconsciously consuming an ad for a diet product or hearing diet culture messaging, which, as we've established, is bad for body image.

TV AS A FORCE FOR GOOD

In the divided society that we currently live in, it's easy to fall into the trap of thinking someone or something is 'good' or 'bad'. But in reality, things are more complicated than that; nuance exists and it's important to recognise that something can have both a negative and a positive impact at the same time. Things are never simple – life's annoying like that.

In 2006 Gok Wan's *How to Look Good Naked* burst onto the screen on Channel 4 and made a huge impact on how millions of women viewed their bodies. 'It happened at a Zeitgeist – it was part of a moment in time when women were fed up of being told what to do, when to do it and how to wear it,' said Gok in an interview on the daytime TV show *Loose Women* in October 2019.[8] That interview was to talk about the new series of the show, resurrected nine years after the first run. And despite the gap in series, Gok told the interviewers the show was needed now more than ever. 'I have to say we are in the worst position we've ever been in with our bodies ever, right now. Social media has a huge part to play. None of the images we see any more are real, they're all doctored. You're comparing yourself to an animation, an illustration. It's impossible for us to look like that.'

Like *How to Look Good Naked*, the show I was on in 2019, *Naked Beach*, was also aired on Channel 4 and also challenged the idea that we shouldn't be allowed to like ourselves just as we are. These shows had a huge impact on millions of people viewing them and catapulted important conversations about body image and the pressure to be perfect directly on to prime-time, mainstream TV.

Just as TV has the power to make kids (and adults) feel bad about their bodies, it has the power to build them up too. It can inspire children and introduce them to new ideas. The animated TV series *Steven Universe*, for Cartoon Network, is another perfect example of this. Created by Rebecca Sugar in 2013, it's the first animated series devised solely by a woman and was critically acclaimed for its prominence of LGBTQ+ themes, inclusion and body positivity. *Steven Universe* was nominated for five Emmys and won multiple awards. In 2018 it teamed up with the Dove Self-Esteem Project to deliver self-esteem and body confidence education in schools (you can find the link to the lesson resources in the Resources section on page 235).

In an interview with Lauren Rearick for *Teen Vogue* magazine at the time, Rebecca Sugar said, 'I feel an immense responsibility to use my platform to help children who are struggling. In my early conversations with Dove my main goal was to make sure that these shorts would be accessible, not just for girls but also gender-expansive kids and boys. I want all children to have access to messages about self-care. To the kids watching for whom this isn't an issue, I want them to gain a better understanding of their fellow kids who are struggling.'[9]

BODY HAPPY KIDS TOOLKIT
Media Literacy

The science

I've worked as a journalist, researcher, producer and presenter in radio, TV, magazines and newspapers and I *still* often fall prey to the negative body image messages in these places, despite knowing all the tricks of the trade to sell a story. Media literacy can help with this though! It's a useful tool for when these messages come our way, and it's something you might find helpful for yourself as well as your kids. Essentially, media literacy lets us take a step back and view what we're seeing with a critical lens so it doesn't hit quite so hard. I like to think of it as a bit like catching a bomb that hasn't yet gone off, unplugging the detonator and throwing it in a bucket of water. Media literacy defuses the message before it can explode and do damage.

Common Sense Media describes media literacy as simply the 'ability to identify different types of media and understand the messages they're sending'.[10] It's about understanding who created the media and why they created it – and it's that 'why' which is at the heart of media literacy.

There's a whole range of research to show that media literacy can help when it comes to body image.[11] There's also evidence to show that parental involvement in helping kids develop these skills can really help, meaning we shouldn't just leave it up to the teachers at school.[12]

The key concepts of media literacy are:

1. All media is constructed.
2. Media messages shape our perception of reality.
3. Different people will have a different understanding of the same message.
4. Media messages have commercial implications.
5. Media messages embed points of view.

Remembering these concepts is important when we get to the tool bit in a second because it's useful to know – and to let our kids know – that media doesn't just appear out of thin air. It's always someone's job to make it, and their own biases, opinions and intentions, as well as the biases, opinions and intentions of the organisation they work for, will shape how that media gets constructed. And these media messages have huge implications for the way we all see the world and our place in it. So, for body image, this might mean that the messages around health will

embed a particular point of view, for example, which might negatively impact how we feel about our bodies.

As well as these key concepts, it's useful to remember that media literacy isn't just something you sit down and do. In fact, the American Academy of Pediatrics, Common Sense Media and the National Association for Media Literacy Education recommend not only keeping TVs and phones out of kids' rooms and away from the dinner table but also to try to actively watch with your kids where you can and have conversations along the way.[13] (Research shows this is an important element of teaching children about Internet safety too.)[14] Easier said than done if you're busy and need to use the iPad babysitter, I know, but even just doing this occasionally can make a big difference.

The tool: a media literacy how-to

You can use this tool with any type of media – a social media post, a TikTok video, a YouTube video, a TV show, a film, an advert, a newspaper article, a magazine feature. Experts say it's best brought into everyday conversations rather than a sit-down activity, but the more you get to discuss these ideas and the sooner you start to have these chats, the more clued up your kids will be when it comes to decoding what they see on screen.

Media literacy starter questions

> » Who made it? (Was it one person or a whole team of people?)
> » Why did they make it? (Was it to sell you something, to inform you, to persuade you to do something or to make you laugh, etc.?)

» Who is it for? (Kids, grown-ups, people who have a particular interest in common?)

» What are they doing to make you believe them? (Have they got statistics? Are they quoting experts? Are they using special music? What kind of imagery are they using? Is there text on the screen, etc.?)

» What did they miss out? (Do they show both sides of the story? What else might they have included?)

» How did it make you feel? (Will others feel this way too? Why did it make you feel this way? Would anyone disagree with you and feel a different way? Why might this be?)

Media literacy tips by age

Pre-schoolers: At this age, it's about teaching children that the media they are seeing has been made by someone – and that it's not real. So start with what they know about what is real and not real. For example, is the princess in this cartoon real or is it just a drawing? Is that monster real or is it make-believe? You can then help children relate this to a real-life scenario and talk about the differences between reality and what they see on TV.

Ages 5–7: At this age, children can start to empathise and learn that not everyone sees and experiences the world in the same way, so this is a great time to have conversations about how others might view a particular subject. This could be as simple as asking them what they think the maker of their favourite YouTube video thinks about a certain toy – and why another child might not agree.

Ages 8–10: This is a brilliant age to start having deeper conversations about the role of media in our culture, and how the videos we watch on YouTube and the things we see on TV might shape our opinions about things.

Tweens: By this age, children should be able to grasp more complicated concepts, such as the impact of 'click bait' and sensationalist headlines. This is a great time to decode some of their favourite videos on YouTube, for example, and talk about how the person making the video has created a title that encourages them to click on it.

Teenagers: You can really get deep with media literacy at this age, and it might lead to some interesting discussions. Teenagers will also be able to discuss bias and recognise how different media cover the same story. Perhaps you could take two opposing newspapers, for example, and look at how they've covered a particular health story or campaign.

CHAPTER 10

The Art of Dress-Up: Clothes, Kids and Body Image

For me, and very possibly for you, the way I have felt about my body in the past has been inextricably linked to the clothes I put on it. Clothes have been the source of playful fun, painful shame and empowering identity exploration. The same is true for children.

Fashion, like social media, often gets accused of promoting unrealistic beauty ideals and perpetuating a culture where body insecurities thrive, but, as I hope you've realised by this point in the book, things are rarely that simple. It's a nuanced subject and, although a single chapter can't cover everything, we're going to peel back some of the layers of the conversation.

From school uniform to the dressing-up box and their first forays into fashion, we're going to hear how the clothes kids wear and the ways we talk about clothes can shape the way children feel about their bodies. At the end of this chapter you'll find a toolkit that will hopefully help to ensure the clothes our kids put on their bodies empower rather than confine them (page 225).

JUST A NUMBER

It was just a number, on a label, on a piece of fabric, sitting alongside practical instructions talking about wash temperatures and iron heats. It was just a number, arbitrary, like the number on my front door or on the page of this very book. It was just a number that I'd learned to draw one day as a child, gripping the pencil with tiny fingers, my tongue protruding from my lips as I concentrated on getting the squiggles the right way round. It was just a number. But it was so much more.

It was the number after childbirth signifying that my body now took up more space. It was the number in adolescence signifying my breasts were still undeveloped. It was the number in my twenties signifying the success or failure of whatever punishing workout or food regime I was trying that week. It was the number that signified my worth. For many of us, the number on a clothes label carries a memory. A memory of something being too small or too big and the shame that came with that. A memory of feeling like your body is wrong. It was never just a number, on a label, on a piece of fabric.

My experience of clothes labels may well be different to yours. Living in the body that I do means I've often been able to find clothes that fit me in most shops. Even if my body does not resemble the tall, thin supermodels on the catwalk, the high street still caters to me, so simply deciding to 'size up' or ignore the label was an option open to me that isn't to

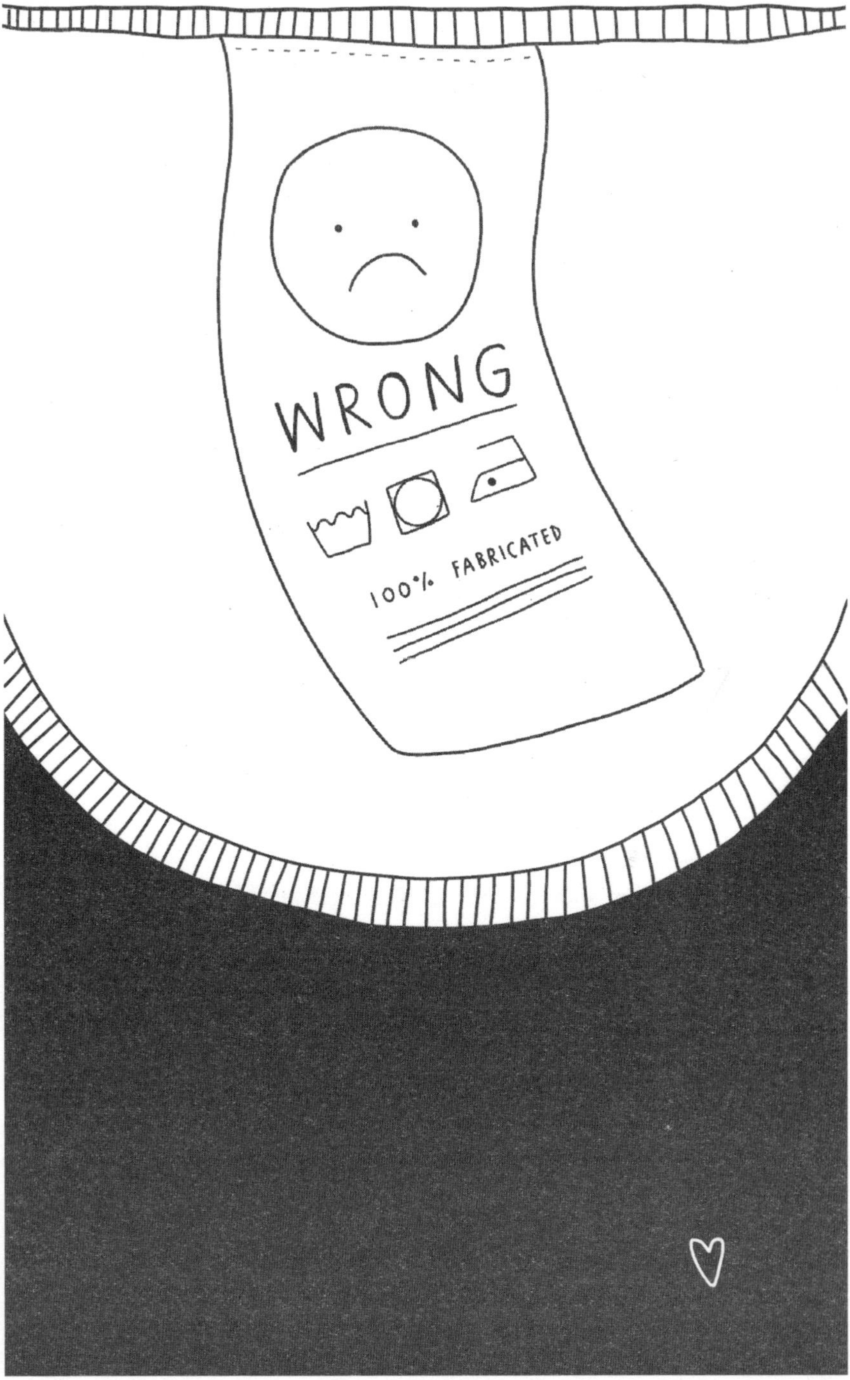
WRONG
100% FABRICATED

many. Conversations about size inclusivity are becoming more common as the fashion industry starts to wake up to the importance of this (although there's no denying there is still a long way to go). But when it comes to kids' clothes, the way the garments are sized, designed and cut can also impact how they learn about their place in the world and how their bodies may need to change to fit these roles. This is what we're going to discuss next.

HOW KIDS' CLOTHES CAN BE BAD NEWS FOR BODY IMAGE

You might think the clothes your children wear have no impact on how they feel about their bodies, other than keeping them warm or cool. But gender stereotypes (which we've already established are bad news for body image) in kids' clothes start from day one, and we're not just talking dinosaurs versus unicorns – it goes right to the sizes of the clothes you pick for your kids.

Liz Kehoe is the founder of Wunderkind + Wild, an independent online brand selling clothes and accessories to help raise funds for mental health charities. Prior to this, Liz worked in luxury fashion in London. 'I occasionally buy some of my sons' clothes from the girls' section of a well-known high-street clothing brand,' says Liz. 'I have to go up two age sizes in the girls' clothes to get the length the same as their own age in the boys. The girls' clothing is often cut shorter and the waist measurements show a cinched-in size for the girls. They copy the format for gendered adult clothing. This is standard unfortunately, and a lot of this comes from the fifties and sixties when the sizing standards were worked out.'

This was the case for four out of five of the big UK high-street kids' brands I checked out. In each of these places the brands carried different sizing measurements for boys and girls between the ages of nine to eleven, with the girls' measurements coming up smaller. You might think this would make sense if, on average, girls were smaller than boys, but the Royal College of Paediatrics and Child Health growth charts (based on the WHO child growth standards) show a different story. According to those charts, between the ages of nine and eleven girls tend to be slightly heavier than boys and by eleven years old the charts show them as slightly taller too. This is likely because girls tend to go through puberty a couple of years earlier than boys and experience a growth spurt around this age. Taking this into account then, you might assume the clothing brands would make girls' sizes at this age slightly *bigger* than the boys' sizes, but the opposite is true, meaning that at the exact age girls' bodies start to change and they are more vulnerable to feeling self-conscious about their shape, they risk being squeezed into clothes that may be too tight. Arguably at this age the label on the clothes carries even more significance – it's not just an arbitrary dress size but a number related to the age of the child, telling us that this is the body we expect a child of this age to have.

The differences don't just boil down to sizing though. The way the clothes are cut is often very different too. Girls' designs are generally more fitted, with tighter sleeves and lower cut necklines, while the boys' designs are looser. Sometimes the material is even different too, with girls' designs made from less durable fabric. And don't even get me started on the lack of pockets.

Why does this matter though? Because it's ultimately perpetuating that age-old idea that little girls' (and women's) bodies are for *being* and little boys' (and men's) bodies are for *doing*. The very clothes on offer to children – right from birth – can reinforce the notion that the job of girls is to sit still and look pretty while the job of boys is to run about and jump in puddles. This can create problems when it comes to body image because not only does it risk girls being objectified, both by themselves and others, but it risks boys feeling like they need to live up to a stereotype of what it means to be a boy – active and strong. And, as we found out earlier from some of the toys that are marketed towards boys, those traits are often equated with having big muscles and a six-pack.

These stereotypes don't just play out in the sizing and the cut of the clothes. They can be seen in the prints on the fabric too. When I was looking at the size guides on those five kids' high-street fashion brands I noticed differences in the designs too. For example, while both the girls' and boys' ranges featured pictures of animals, the girls' designs were adorned with bunny rabbits, squirrels and cats, while the boys' were decorated with lions, crocodiles and bears. The message is pretty clear: girls are all about the cute and fluffy, while boys are about the fierce and strong. It's the same case for the patterns too, with the girls' ranges often covered in hearts, flowers and rainbows, while the boys' ranges are decked out in camouflage, stripes or checks. You could read some deep symbolism into this; in a culture where little girls are often raised to take on the brunt of emotional labour and be caring and loving it can't be a coincidence that their clothes are adorned with the very symbol of love. Meanwhile, the boys' clothes are covered with designs reflecting the role society traditionally gives men: the strong protector, the fierce hunter-gatherer. There's no room for feelings here.

You might think this is a far reach but a study in 2012 found that the clothes we wear can affect the way we behave.[1] In this study the researchers investigated how wearing a lab coat affected performance on attention-related tasks, after a pre-test found a lab coat is generally associated with attentiveness and carefulness. The results showed 'a systematic influence that clothes have on the wearer's psychological processes' – which the researchers named 'enclothed cognition'. In the first experiment they found that selective attention increased when people were wearing the lab coat, compared with wearing no coat at all. They also tested to see if telling the participants that the coat was a 'lab coat' or a 'painter's coat' had any effect – and it did! When people were wearing what they believed was the lab coat their selective attention increased compared to when people were wearing the coat that they believed to be a painter's coat.

I'm not suggesting that putting a kid in a top with a lion on it will turn that child into a fierce predator, but the enclothed cognition theory does lend some weight to the argument that continually choosing clothes that perpetuate gender stereotypes for children might affect the way they behave and see their roles in the world, which in turn can affect how they feel about their bodies. Clothes are more than just a piece of fabric.

FASHION AS A TOOL FOR EMPOWERMENT

If you've come to the conclusion that I hate fashion, then you'd be wrong. I love clothes and have always derived a special kind of thrill from a new outfit. Whether it was my favourite cycling short and skirt combo as a kid in the nineties or just discovering the joy of dungarees as a fully grown adult, I get a lot of pleasure from clothes – and my kids do too.

My friend Jsky is someone who also appreciates the power of fashion. As well as being a TV and radio host (we first met working on *Naked Beach* together), Jsky is also a singer-songwriter, fashionista and self-love activist. For Jsky, clothes have become a tool to express his identity and unapologetically take up space in the world.

'I've always seen how you dress as the way you want to present yourself to the world,' says Jsky. 'I was taught to dress for the position that you want in life. For me personally that was a singer, so I always used to dress as if I was on a big stage. I like attention, so I like to wear things that are a bit over the top. I'm of the mindset that kids should be free to get creative if they want, and to wear clothes that make them happy, because certain clothing makes us feel a certain way – but that doesn't necessarily mean we *are* a certain way. There are some great examples of celebrities who have learned this very publicly; people such as Lewis Hamilton telling his nephew that he shouldn't wear a dress but later learning it's not that big a deal, for example.[2] We should be free to wear anything that makes us happy, and if the children in our life want to wear a certain thing and it makes us uncomfortable then maybe that's on us and not on the child. We shouldn't push our limited views, which have been created by a world filled with judgement and prejudice, on a child.'

This might sound easier said than done. It's a natural instinct to want to protect our kids, which might mean encouraging them to make clothing choices based on conforming to prevent them being singled out or bullied by peers. Social rejection is real and can be painful. As mentioned earlier, research shows that when humans experience social rejection the same part of the brain lights up as when we experience pain.[3] But instead of using this as an argument to encourage our kids to conform through their clothing choices, Jsky says we should be using it as an argument to encourage greater acceptance of others.

'Instead of asking the question of should a child be allowed to wear something they want to wear, the question should really be why does it make us uncomfortable,' says Jsky. 'And that comes from our own insecurities and our own fears, which are often based on the things that we've been told or the things we've seen in society. What I wear is part of my activism. If I'm going to get photographed then I want it to say something; it's a form of rebellion. For me, it's about standing proud and confident and showing I can wear anything. As a kid, I used to battle with wanting to conform. I didn't want to put a target on my back and say, "Look, I'm different." But I've discovered that expressionism is so rewarding – and they say risk-takers live longer! Perhaps if I'd seen someone like me as a role model growing up I'd have realised this sooner. I think our job as parents, as support systems, as allies, as people in this world for the next generation, should be to encourage people to just be themselves and to be there for them no matter what they decide to wear.'

Jsky isn't alone in viewing the clothes he puts on his body as a form of activism and assertion of his identity. In their essay in the book *Disability Visibility*, fashion designer and founder of adaptive and gender non-confirming clothing brand Rebirth Garments, Sky Cubacub, talks about how the clothes they design are deliberately bright with colourful patterns, as well as serving specific functional needs: 'In the face of what society tells us to hide, we are unapologetic individuals who want to celebrate and highlight our bodies. Instead of hiding the aspects of our identities that make us unique, we are Radically Visible.'[4]

Clothes, then, can be a powerful tool in self-expression and give children (and adults) the chance to explore and assert their identity. More than that though, clothes can also be an opportunity for children to learn about consent, namely that their bodies are their own. This is where things get really interesting.

Clothes as a tool to learn about consent

My youngest daughter has always had clear ideas about what she wants to wear. As a toddler she'd want to wear a tutu and wellies to pre-school, and later, aged five, when confined by school uniform, she'd find a way to stand out by wearing every clip, bow and sparkly hairband in her hair. She loves to cut up her old clothes to make new ones, fashioning vests and shorts out of holey tops and leggings, and creates fun combinations, teaming a pair of old evening gloves out of the fancy dress box with a pair of sunglasses and a Christmas jumper. She even wore a waist-length blonde wig to the library once. When I'd suggest the polka dot wellies, leotard and glittery tights weren't the best outfit for the park she'd shout, 'MY BODY, MY RULES!' and how could I argue with that?

At every point my hesitation in allowing her to wear what she wanted came from a place of protection – I didn't want her to be cold, I didn't want her to be laughed at by people in the library or, more shamefully, I didn't want my own judgement as a mother to be questioned.

Victoria Welsby, who we heard from in the last chapter, says this is a slippery slope: 'By policing the clothes your kids are wearing – even if it comes with the intention of protection –

you're doing the exact same thing, if not worse than, the playground bullies are doing, because your kids love you and respect you and want your approval.'

Parents can try to police their kids' outfit choices for all sorts of reasons, but Victoria warns that if you're suggesting your child shouldn't wear a particular outfit because of the shape of their body – even if you are well-meaning – you may do some serious damage. 'By telling your child not to wear a certain outfit because you don't think it's flattering, you're doing the exact same thing you're scared is going to happen to them in the playground; you're telling them their body is not OK and they shouldn't be wearing that. And if there is bullying because of the outfit choice of your child, then you need to deal with the fact the bullying shouldn't have happened, not the clothes wearing.'

Telling your child not to wear certain clothes to avoid being bullied is, says Victoria, equivalent to telling a woman not to wear a short skirt to avoid being sexually harassed. It's the same train of victim-blaming thought, when in fact we should be challenging the source of the abuse in the first place.

This is a big task, particularly for parents of girls, who will need to battle against all sorts of ingrained ideas about what is 'respectable' or 'acceptable'. These ideas are reinforced everywhere, even in the way school uniform policies are written and enforced. Many schools will specify that girls need to wear skirts or pinafore dresses, for example, while boys can wear shorts or trousers. This goes back to the differences in the messages we give kids about what their bodies are for, but also speaks to the way we teach girls to police their bodies for the approval of others. I often get messages from parents of teenage girls on social media who are conflicted because their daughter's been told off for wearing a top that is 'too tight' or a skirt that is 'too short', for example. These attitudes might seem like they're empowering young girls to avoid objectification, but they also risk drawing even more attention to growing girls' bodies. We need to ask ourselves – would this girl still be told off for her outfit choices if she had a different-shaped body? Would that tight top be seen as more acceptable if the girl's breasts were smaller, for example? I've come to feel now that instead of teaching young girls to be vigilant over the way they present their bodies, we should be teaching young boys not to view girls' bodies as objects to be looked at in the first place.

If we create an environment where all bodies are seen as good bodies and where children are encouraged to believe their worth lies beyond the outward appearance of their bodies, then it stands to reason they'll be more likely to find a joyful relationship with clothes later on. Maybe this way, they'll genuinely choose outfits that make them feel good.

Of course, this is all hugely personal and the cultural context along with your own lived experiences will all play a role in how you approach the clothes your child puts on their body. And the clothing industry has a huge part to play here too. But hopefully this might give another perspective to this vast and nuanced subject. For me, personally, if in doubt I follow the lead of my daughters, who tell me, regularly, 'My body, my rules!'

BODY HAPPY KIDS TOOLKIT

How to Help Kids Feel Empowered in their Clothes

The science

Remember that cool term 'enclothed cognition' we talked about earlier? Let's go back to it for a second. It's a term coined by cognitive psychologists Hajo Adam and Adam Galinsky in their research study with the lab coat in 2012 (see page 219) and it's related to how the clothes we wear affect the way we think and feel. They proved that power dressing is more than just a catchy marketing slogan.

The results of their study have been backed up by other research which shows our clothing choices can impact our mental agility too, with various studies showing tight clothes and clothes that make us more aware of our bodies can affect how we perform on tasks and how we feel about our bodies.[5] Experts think this is likely because the brain space (or 'cognitive resources') needed to focus on the task in hand are taken up with thinking about the body.

For children, the research is hazier. There's some evidence to show, for example, that some neurodivergent children sometimes prefer to wear tight clothing.[6] Equally, other children are more comfortable in baggier, looser clothes. While for some kids feeling the seams on socks and underwear can be a real source of distress. Essentially, researchers can't investigate the impact of tight clothes and how this may cause self-objectification with children because of ethical limitations in how they'd design the study.

Put simply, there is no one-size-fits-all approach to clothing and kids. We do know, though, that how clothes fit can impact how we feel in our bodies, and that gender stereotypes can be bad news for body image too. We're going to put some of this knowledge into action now and look at ways we can help kids make clothing choices that empower them and make them feel good.

The toolkit: a smart shopping guide

I've called this toolkit a 'smart shopping guide' but this doesn't mean it needs to be restricted to the moments you actually go shopping (both in physical stores and online). These ideas can come into play when you're 'shopping your wardrobe', as the fashion influencers say, or when you're sourcing any clothes for your kids, whether they're new-new or new-to-you (i.e. pre-loved).

This is not written as a rigid rulebook you must follow to the letter, but rather a source of inspiration to help you and your child navigate their sartorial choices together. Take a picture and keep it on your phone ready for the next shopping trip or wardrobe battle – think of it as a pep talk from me to you the next time a kids' clothing crisis hits.

1. Ditch the label

There's no rule that says boys need to wear clothes from the boys' section and girls need to wear clothes from the girls' section. It's your money; you can spend it where you like. The next time you go shopping for your kid it might be interesting to have a look in the other part of the store too. Remember, the way clothes are designed is often different for boys and girls, so you might need to experiment with the sizes to find which one fits best. Speaking of which, there's also no rule to say that you need to stick to the size that is the age for your child. If this is a potential trigger point for your kids then it might help to remove the label altogether.

2. The comfort test

A great tip for trying on clothes is to close your eyes and consider what the outfit feels like against your skin before you look in the mirror. This is a good one for kids too, particularly older children and teenagers. Even if your child ends up hating the outfit at least you'll get a good sense of how comfortable they find it before they see what it looks like on their body.

3. Acceptance over judgement

Some kids are happy to wear the clothes their parents pick out for them and some are not. If your child has a clear idea of what they like to wear, go with it. Think of this as a teachable moment about consent ('My body, my rules!') and a chance for your child to explore who they are and what they like.

4. Affirmations are your friend

It's an affirmation all over Instagram, but it can be a useful way to frame how we think about clothes: *It's the clothes' job to fit your body, not your body's job to fit the clothes.* Our bodies change all the time and they have far more important things to do than prioritise fitting into a piece of fabric. This can be a particularly useful thing to remind kids going through puberty or experiencing a growth spurt, and it can take the sting out of a changing room moment if something doesn't fit.

A Body Happy Future

I want to end this book on a high. I want you to feel empowered to help your kids feel good in their bodies and take on diet culture, armed with knowledge and tools and a new-found enthusiasm to challenge the mainstream narratives that may make them question their bodies and, by extension, their worth in the world. But I'm going to be honest: it's not going to be easy.

It should not be a radical idea that all children have the right to feel good about their bodies. Unfortunately though too many people, industries and power structures are invested in us not feeling good, meaning we can't free our children (and ourselves) from appearance ideals without a fight. But it is a fight we must take on.

It starts with difficult conversations. Difficult conversations with some of the people in your life you might be closest to;

maybe even difficult conversations with yourself. If you, like me, are a people-pleaser who hates conflict, then I understand this will be hard. But through difficult conversations we can create change.

Difficult conversations look like this:

» Challenging normalised weight stigma from family members at the dinner table.
» Being *that parent* who emails the head teacher if you see a diet ad on the school gates.
» Asking your friend not to comment on that celebrity's weight loss or 'body transformation' in front of your children.

It might also look like refusing to engage in diet chat in the office or pledging to try non-appearance-based compliments the next time you catch up with someone you haven't seen in a while.

This stuff is messy and often uncomfortable, but we must do it, because if we don't advocate for the children in our life then who will?

I am not suggesting you need to march up and down your street with a megaphone or start raging debates in the school playground. Experience has taught me that, even armed with the stats and the studies, if people aren't ready to listen then you can't make them. No one wants to be lectured to – least of all our kids. But what you can do is appeal to people's love for your children.

It's likely the people with whom these conversations are most important are the ones who are an intrinsic part of your life – family members, teachers, friends. Like you, these people want the best for your child. Tell them how it might make your child feel if they hear that casual fatphobia at the dinner table or in the classroom. Perhaps this stuff has caused you personal pain in the past too, so you can speak from experience.

We are not born hating our bodies, and with you advocating for them, your precious, brilliant, unique child has the chance to be truly body happy. We don't need to settle for the alternative and accept the path we are currently on towards raising a generation of kids ashamed of their bodies. Change is possible, and we are part of the solution.

We can do it. They're counting on us.

Further Support and Resources

If reading this book has brought up some uncomfortable feelings for you or it's made you realise that perhaps you need help with some of the topics discussed within these pages, either for yourself or your child, then please know that there *is* help out there.

ONLINE SUPPORT

Beat, the UK's leading eating disorder charity, can be found at beateatingdisorders.org.uk

Childline has online advice regarding children and body image, with a 24-hour helpline on 0800 1111 and an online counsellor chat service at childline.org.uk

Mental health services directory the Hub of Hope can be found at hubofhope.co.uk

Rethink Mental Illness is a provider of mental health services in England and can be found at rethink.org

The Children's Society has online resources and local drop-in centres for young people in some parts of the UK and can be found at childrenssociety.org.uk

The Mix is a UK charity providing free confidential support for young people under 25 and can be found at themix.org.uk

Young Minds offers guidance for young people struggling with self-esteem and has a parent support helpline on 0808 802 5544 and online resources at youngminds.org.uk

BOOKS FOR CHILDREN AND TEENAGERS

» *Celebrate Your Body* by Sonya Renee Taylor (Rockridge Press, 2018)
» *Her Body Can* by Katie Crenshaw and Ady Meschke (East 26th Publishing, 2020)
» *I Am Not a Label* by Cerrie Burnell (Wide Eyed Editions, 2020)
» *It Isn't Rude to be Nude* by Rosie Haine (Tate Publishing, 2020)
» *It's Okay to be Different* by Todd Parr (Little, Brown, 2009)
» *Jemima Small Versus the Universe* by Tamsin Winter (Usborne Publishing, 2019)

» *Love Your Body* by Jessica Sanders
(Frances Lincoln, 2020)

» *Shapesville* by Andy Mills and Becky Osborn
(Gurze Books, 2003)

» *The Body Image Book for Girls* by Charlotte Markey
(Cambridge University Press, 2020)

» *The Second Life of Abigail Walker* by Frances O'Roark Dowell
(Atheneum Books for Young Readers, 2013)

» *What I Like About Me!* by Allia Zobel-Nolan
(Reader's Digest Association, 2009)

» *You Are Enough* by Harri Rose
(Aster, 2019)

» *You Matter* by Christian Robinson
(Simon & Schuster, 2020)

» *Your Body is Brilliant* by Sigrun Danielsdottir
(Singing Dragon, 2014)

CLASSROOM RESOURCES

The Be Real Campaign 'Body Confidence Toolkit for Schools'
can be found at https://www.berealcampaign.co.uk/resources/
body-confidence-campaign-toolkit-for-schools

The Dove Self-Esteem Project x *Steven Universe* for the Cartoon
Network http://www.stevenuniverseselfesteem.co.uk

You can also find further workshops, downloadable materials and resources for parents and teachers at The Body Happy
Organisation, the community interest company I founded to
promote positive body image in kids, at bodyhappyorg.com

EXTRA RESOURCES BY CHAPTER

Chapter 1

Canva and PicMonkey are two free graphic design websites you can use to make affirmations in the toolkit in this chapter.

Chapter 3

Social Farms & Gardens is a UK-wide charity supporting communities to farm and grow together. Find one near you at farmgarden.org.uk

Mush and Peanut are two apps to help you connect with other parents.

Cosmic Kids is a yoga YouTube channel for children which features kid-friendly meditation sessions.

The Headspace app also has a kids' meditation tool.

Chapter 6

For fun, free and diet-culture-free kids' movement sessions, check out the following YouTube channels: Cosmic Kids, GoNoodle, Just Dance and Koo Koo Kanga Roo.

Parkrun is a global free running movement and takes place in parks all over the world. Saturday morning events are 5k and Sunday morning events are 2k junior park runs for kids aged 4–14.

Chapter 8

Look out for the Lottie doll range, which challenges gender stereotypes and unrealistic body ideals.

★

Finally, if you're interested in finding out more about this huge subject, I highly recommend seeking out the work of the researchers, authors, activists and educators quoted and cited within this book.

Acknowledgements

This book was written in 2020, started as the UK went into lockdown and completed as I was self-isolating. When I was a young girl dreaming of writing a book, I imagined I would be in a log cabin by a peaceful lake somewhere, not writing while simultaneously home-schooling two children and working full-time with my day job. But I did it, and this is largely due to the huge support I have had from my husband, Si, and my mum and dad, Ghislaine and Simon. Without them, this book probably wouldn't exist.

There have been many tears and moments of imposter syndrome which have almost prevented the words hitting the page, at which point my sister Lizzy has been there to cheer me on, as have my parents-in-law, Maggie and Steve.

I also want to give special thanks to my talented friends, Sarah Turner and Alison Perry, for offering a huge amount of practical advice throughout. Their wisdom is gold and I owe them wine and cake forever.

There are so many people in my life who have listened to me rant about diet culture and its impact on children, have encouraged me to do something about it, and helped me believe that I could write this book. Their messages, WhatsApps, calls and talks have helped me more than they'll ever know (you know who you are).

I owe special thanks to every person who gave up their time to contribute their insights to this book. The many interviews on Zoom and email conversations made the process less lonely and have shaped this book into what it is. I'm also indebted to the amazing people who have forged a conversation on this subject already with their books, podcasts, research and social media accounts. Thank you for the work that you do; it is needed and appreciated.

Thanks also to my agent, Lauren Gardner, for being so brilliant and supportive, my commissioning editor, Sam Jackson and the team at Vermilion, for believing in this book and my ability to write it, and my copy editor, Julia Kellaway, for challenging me on parts of the book, making me think about other perspectives and tidying up my very messy references section. And thanks to Anya Hayes, the very first person in the world of publishing to give me hope that the idea in my head could – and needed to – exist in book form.

And, finally, thank you to my daughters, Freya and Effie. You told me I could do it, you believed in me, and I hope I've done you proud.

Endnotes

Introduction

1 Petkova, H., Simic, M., Nicholls, D., Ford, T., Prina, A. M., Stuart, R., Livingstone, N., Kelly, G., Macdonald, G., Eisler, I. and Gowers, S., 2019. 'Incidence of anorexia nervosa in young people in the UK and Ireland: A national surveillance study.' *BMJ Open*, *9*(10), p. e027339.

2 Halliwell, E., Diedrichs, C. and Orbach, S., 2014. 'Costing the invisible: A review of the evidence examining the links between body image, aspirations, education and workplace confidence.' Centre for Appearance Research, University of the West of England [technical report]; The Mental Health Foundation, 13 May 2019. 'Body image: How we think and feel about our bodies.' Retrieved from https://www.mentalhealth.org.uk/publications/body-image-report.

3 Fredrickson, B. L. and Roberts, T. A., 1997. 'Objectification theory: Toward understanding women's lived experiences and mental health risks.' *Psychology of Women Quarterly*, 21(2), pp. 173–206; Gillen, M. M., 2015. 'Associations between positive body image and indicators of men's and women's mental and physical health.' *Body Image*, 13, pp. 67–74

Chapter 1

1 Kenny, E. and Nichols, E. G., 2017. *Beauty Around the World: A Cultural Encyclopedia*. ABC-CLIO.

2 Fredrickson, B. L. and Roberts, T. A., 1997. 'Objectification theory: Toward understanding women's lived experiences and mental health risks.' *Psychology of Women Quarterly*, *21*(2), pp. 173–206.

3 Kristen-Antonow, S., Sodian, B., Perst, H. and Licata, M., 2015. 'A longitudinal study of the emerging self from 9 months to the age of 4 years.' *Frontiers in Psychology*, 6, p. 789.

4 Professional Association for Childcare and Early Years, 31 Aug. 2016. 'Children as young as 3 unhappy with their bodies.' Retrieved from https://www.pacey.org.uk/news-and-views/news/archive/2016-news/august-2016/children-as-young-as-3-unhappy-with-their-bodies/.

5 Damiano, S. R., Paxton, S. J., Wertheim, E. H., McLean, S. A. and Gregg, K. J., 2015. 'Dietary restraint of 5-year-old girls: Associations with internalization of the thin ideal and maternal, media, and peer influences. *International Journal of Eating Disorders*, *48*(8), pp. 1166–9.

6   Common Sense Media, 21 Jan. 2015. 'Children, teens, media and
      body image.' Retrieved from https://www.commonsensemedia.org/
      research/children-teens-media-and-body-image.
7   Professional Association for Childcare and Early Years, 31 Aug.
      2016. 'Children as young as 3 unhappy with their bodies.'
      Retrieved from https://www.pacey.org.uk/news-and-views/
      news/archive/2016-news/august-2016/
      children-as-young-as-3-unhappy-with-their-bodies/.
8   BBC Newsround, 28 Aug. 2019. 'Good Childhood Report: Almost
      a quarter of a million UK children "unhappy".' Retrieved from
      https://www.bbc.co.uk/newsround/49487510; The Children's
      Society, 2019. 'The Good Childhood Report, 2019.' Retrieved from
      https://saphna.co/wp-content/uploads/2019/11/the_good_child-
      hood_report_2019.pdf.
9   Brennan, M. A., Lalonde, C. E. and Bain, J. L., 2010. 'Body
      image perceptions: Do gender differences exist?' *Psi Chi Journal of
      Undergraduate Research*, *15*(3), pp. 130–8; Burlew, L. D. and Shurts,
      W. M., 2013. 'Men and body image: Current issues and counseling
      implications.' *Journal of Counseling & Development*, *91*(4), pp. 428–35;
      Bandura, A., 1969. *Principles of Behavior Modification*. Holt, Rinehart
      & Winston.
10   Chaplin, T. M., Cole, P. M. and Zahn-Waxler, C., 2005. 'Parental
      socialization of emotion expression: Gender differences and relations
      to child adjustment.' *Emotion*, *5*(1), p. 80.
11   Stipek, D. J., Gralinski, J. H. and Kopp, C. B., 1990. 'Self-concept
      development in the toddler years.' *Developmental Psychology*, *26*(6),
      pp. 972–7.
12   The Mental Health Foundation, 13 May 2019. 'Body image: How
      we think and feel about our bodies.' Retrieved from https://www.
      mentalhealth.org.uk/publications/body-image-report.
13   Girlguiding UK, 2017. 'Girls' attitudes survey.' Retrieved from
      https://www.girlguiding.org.uk/globalassets/docs-and-resources/
      research-and-campaigns/girls-attitudes-survey-2017.pdf.
14   Ramseyer Winter, V., Kennedy, A. K. and O'Neill, E., 2017.
      'Adolescent tobacco and alcohol use: The influence of body image.'
      Journal of Child & Adolescent Substance Abuse, *26*(3), pp. 219–28.
15   Halliwell, E., Diedrichs, P. C. and Orbach, S., 2014. 'Costing the
      invisible: A review of the evidence examining the links between
      body image, aspirations, education and workplace confidence.'
      Centre for Appearance Research, University of the West of England
      [technical report].
16   World Health Organization, 2017. 'Weight bias and obesity stigma:
      Considerations for the WHO European Region.' Retrieved from
      https://www.euro.who.int/en/health-topics/noncommunicable-

diseases/obesity/publications/2017/weight-bias-and-obesity-stigma-considerations-for-the-who-european-region-2017.

17   The Lancet Public Health, 2019. 'Addressing weight stigma.' *The Lancet Public Health,* *4*(4), p. e168.

18   Personnel Today, 25 Oct. 2005. 'Obesity research: Fattism is the last bastion of employee discrimination.' Retrieved from https://www.personneltoday.com/hr/obesity-research-fattism-is-the-last-bastion-of-employee-discrimination/.

19   Mintel, Feb. 2016. 'Attitudes towards healthy eating – UK.' Retrieved from https://store.mintel.com/report/attitudes-towards-healthy-eating-uk-february-2016.

20   Modern Aesthetics, 19 May 2019. '2018 BAAPS Data: Liposuction up by 9 percent in 2018.' https://modernaesthetics.com/news/2018-baaps-data-liposuction-up-by-9-percent-in-2018.

21   Bergstrom, R. L., Neighbours, C. and Malheim, J. E., 2009. 'Media comparisons and threats to body image: Seeking evidence of self-affirmation. *Journal of Social and Clinical Psychology, 28*(2), pp. 264–80.

22   Webb, J. B., Rogers, C. B., Etzel, L. and Padro, M. P., 2018. '"Mom, quit fat talking – I'm trying to eat (mindfully) here!": Evaluating a sociocultural model of family fat talk, positive body image, and mindful eating in college women.' *Appetite, 126,* pp. 169–75.

23   Michael, S. L., Wentzel, K., Elliott, M. N., Dittus, P. J., Kanouse, D. E., Wallander, J. L., Pasch, K. E., Franzini, L., Taylor, W. C., Qureshi, T. and Franklin, F. A., 2014. 'Parental and peer factors associated with body image discrepancy among fifth-grade boys and girls.' *Journal of Youth and Adolescence, 43*(1), pp. 15–29.

Chapter 2

1   Be Real, 17 Jan. 2017. 'Somebody like me: A report investigating the impact of body image anxiety in young people in the UK.' Retrieved from https://www.berealcampaign.co.uk/research/somebody-like-me.

2   Strings, S., 2019. *Fearing the Black Body.* New York University Press.

3   Mardsen, R., 11 Dec. 2015. ' The first coin-operated scales: Rhodri Mardsen's interesting objects no. 91.' *Independent.* Retrieved from https://www.independent.co.uk/life-style/gadgets-and-tech/features/the-first-coin-operated-scales-rhodri-marsdens-interesting-objects-no91-a6764391.html.

4   Steele, C. K., 2020. 'American penny scales: A century of ingenuity and design 1891–1991.' Retrieved from https://www.theamericanweigh.com/.

5   Bivins, R. and Marland, H., 2016. 'Weighting for health: Management, measurement and self-surveillance in the modern household.' *Social History of Medicine, 29*(4), pp. 757–80.

6   Markets Insider, 31 Oct. 2019. 'Global weight management market report 2019: Industry trends, share, size, growth, opportunity and forecasts, 2011–2018 & 2019–2024.' Retrieved from https://markets.businessinsider.com/news/stocks/global-weight-management-market-report-2019-industry-trends-share-size-growth-opportunity-and-forecasts-2011-2018-2019-2024-1028647933; Markets Insider, 24 Jul. 2019. 'Weight loss and weight management market worth $245.51 billion by 2022 – Exclusive report by MarketsandMarkets™.' Retrieved from https://markets.businessinsider.com/news/stocks/weight-loss-and-weight-management-market-worth-245-51-billion-by-2022-exclusive-report-by-marketsandmarkets-1028380922.

7   Slimming World, 16 Oct. 2020. 'Terms of use.' Retrieved from https://www.slimmingworld.co.uk/terms-of-use; Weight Watchers. 'If you're an adolescent … ' Retrieved from https://www.weight-watchers.com/uk/article/adolescents.

8   Ducharme, J., 13 Aug. 2019. 'Weight loss for kids? Thanks to WW, There's an app for that.' *Time*. Retrieved from https://time.com/5649964/kurbo-by-ww-app/; Perez, S., 14 Aug. 2019. 'WW launches Kurbo, a hotly debated "healthy eating" app aimed at kids.' TechCrunch. Retrieved from https://techcrunch.com/2019/08/14/ww-launches-kurbo-a-hotly-debated-healthy-eating-app-aimed-at-kids/.

9   Ducharme, J., 13 Aug. 2019. 'Weight loss for kids? Thanks to WW, There's an app for that.' *Time*. Retrieved from https://time.com/5649964/kurbo-by-ww-app/; Mull, A., 20 Aug. 2019. 'Putting Kids on Diets Won't Solve Anything', *The Atlantic*. Retrieved from https://www.theatlantic.com/health/archive/2019/08/weight-watchers-diet-app-kids/596422/.

10   Anderson, J. W., Konz, E. C., Frederich, R. C. and Wood, C. L., 2001. 'Long-term weight-loss maintenance: A meta-analysis of US studies.' *The American Journal of Clinical Nutrition*, 74(5), pp. 579–84.

11   Thomas, L., 2019. *Just Eat It*. Bluebird.

12   McEvedy, S. M., Sullivan-Mort, G., McLean, S. A., Pascoe, M. C. and Paxton, S. J., 2017. 'Ineffectiveness of commercial weight-loss programs for achieving modest but meaningful weight loss: Systematic review and meta-analysis.' *Journal of Health Psychology*, 22(12), pp. 1614–27.

13   iHealthcareAnalyst, Inc., 22 Jan. 2020. 'Global cosmetic surgery and procedures market $50.5 billion by 2027.' Retrieved from https://www.ihealthcareanalyst.com/global-cosmetic-surgery-procedures-market/.

14   British Association of Aesthetic Plastic Surgeons, 20 May 2019.
      'Cosmetic surgery stats: Number of surgeries remains stable amid
      calls for greater regulation of quick fix solutions.' Retrieved from
      https://baaps.org.uk/about/news/1708/cosmetic_surgery_stats_
      number_of_surgeries_remains_stable_amid_calls_for_greater_
      regulation_of_quick_fix_solutions.

15   Girlguiding UK, 2019. 'Girls' attitudes survey.' Retrieved from
      https://www.girlguiding.org.uk/globalassets/docs-and-resources/
      research-and-campaigns/girls-attitudes-survey-2019.pdf.

16   Credos, 2016. 'Picture of health?' Retrieved from http://www.
      adassoc.org.uk/wp-content/uploads/2016/08/Picture-of-health_
      FINAL.pdf.

17   *Business Wire*, 25 Feb. 2019. 'The $72 billion weight loss & diet
      control market in the United States 2019–2023 – Why meal replace-
      ments are still booming but not OTC diet pills.' Retrieved from
      https://www.businesswire.com/news/home/20190225005455/en/
      The-72-Billion-Weight-Loss-Diet-Control-Market-in-the-United-
      States-2019-2023.

18   Crabbe, M. J., 2017. *Body Positive Power: How to stop dieting, make
      peace with your body and live.* Vermilion.

19   Lovato, D., 6 Sep. 2019. Instagram post. Retrieved from https://
      www.instagram.com/p/B2DLlZ4BfgP/?hl=en.

20   Spanos, B., 22 Jan. 2020. 'The joy of Lizzo.' *Rolling Stone*. Retrieved
      from https://www.rollingstone.com/music/music-features/
      lizzo-cover-story-interview-truth-hurts-grammys-937009/.

21   BBC News, 19 Sep. 2019. 'Instagram clamps down on diet and
      cosmetic surgery posts.' Retrieved from https://www.bbc.co.uk/
      news/technology-49746065.

22   Dove. 'Welcome to the Dove self-esteem project.' Retrieved from
      https://www.dove.com/uk/dove-self-esteem-project.html.

23   The Be Real Campaign. 'Body confidence campaign toolkit for
      schools.' Retrieved from https://www.berealcampaign.co.uk/
      resources/body-confidence-campaign-toolkit-for-schools.

24   Davidson, J. E. and Sternberg, R. J., 2012. *The Psychology of Problem
      Solving.* Cambridge University Press.

Chapter 3

1   Crawford, R., 1980. 'Healthism and the medicalization of
     everyday life.' *International Journal of Health Services*, *10*(3),
     pp. 365–88.

2   Lee, J. and Macdonald, D., 2010. '"Are they just checking our
     obesity or what?" The healthism discourse and rural young women.'
     Sport, Education and Society, *15*(2), pp. 203–19.

3   Kolderup Hervik, S. E., 2016. '"Good health is to have a good life":
    How middle-aged and elderly men in a rural town in Norway talk
    about health.' *International Journal of Men's Health*, *15*(3), pp. 218–34.

4   Komaroff, M., 2016. 'For researchers on obesity: Historical review
    of extra body weight definitions.' *Journal of Obesity*, *2016*.

5   Bonthuis, M., Jager, K. J., Abu-Hanna, A., Verrina, E., Schaefer, F.
    and van Stralen, K. J., 2013. 'Application of body mass index
    according to height-age in short and tall children.' *PLoS One*, *8*(8),
    p. e72068.

6   Hudda, M. T., Nightingale, C. M., Donin, A. S., Fewtrell, M. S.,
    Haroun, D., Lum, S., Williams, J. E., Owen, C. G., Rudnicka, A.
    R., Wells, J. C., Cook, D. G. and Whincup, P. H., 2017. 'Body mass
    index adjustments to increase the validity of body fatness assessment
    in UK Black African and South Asian children.' *International Journal
    of Obesity*, *41*(7), pp. 1048–55.

7   Tara, S., 2016. *The Secret Life of Fat*. Blink Publishing; Smith, W. and
    Mukhopadhyay, R., 2012. 'Essential fatty acids: The work of George
    and Mildred Burr.' *The Journal of Biological Chemistry*, *287*(42),
    pp. 35439–41.

8   Osman, A. F., Mehra, M. R., Lavie, C. J., Nunez, E. and Milani,
    R. V., 2000. 'The incremental prognostic importance of body fat
    adjusted peak oxygen consumption in chronic heart failure.' *Journal
    of the American College of Cardiology*, *36*(7), pp. 2126–31; Lavie, C.
    J., 20 May 2014. 'Straight talk: Defending the obesity paradox and
    conflicts of interest.' American College of Cardiology. Retrieved
    from https://www.acc.org/latest-in-cardiology/articles/2014/
    05/20/14/38/straight-talk-defending-the-obesity-paradox-and-
    conflicts-of-interest.

9   Flegal, K. M., Kit, B. K., Orpana, H. and Graubard, B. I., 2013.
    'Association of all-cause mortality with overweight and obesity
    using standard body mass index categories: A systematic review and
    meta-analysis.' *JAMA*, *309*(1), pp. 71–82.

10 *Nature*, 22 May 2013. 'Shades of grey.' Retrieved from https://www.
    nature.com/news/shades-of-grey-1.13029.

11 Catford, J., 1 Dec. 2011. 'Ottawa 1986: Back to the future.' Oxford
    Academic. Retrieved from https://academic.oup.com/heapro/
    article/26/suppl_2/ii163/585303; World Health Organization.
    'The 1st international conference on health promotion, Ottawa,
    1986.' Retrieved from https://www.who.int/healthpromotion/
    conferences/previous/ottawa/en/.

12 Andrew, R., Tiggemann, M. and Clark, L., 2016. 'Predictors and
    health-related outcomes of positive body image in adolescent girls:
    A prospective study.' *Developmental Psychology*, *52*(3), p. 463;

Swami, V., Weis, L., Barron, D. and Furnham, A., 2018. 'Positive body image is positively associated with hedonic (emotional) and eudaimonic (psychological and social) well-being in British adults.' *The Journal of Social Psychology*, *158*(5), pp. 541–52; Gillen, M. M., 2015. 'Associations between positive body image and indicators of men's and women's mental and physical health.' *Body Image*, *13*, pp. 67–74; Neves, C. M., Cipriani, F. M., Meireles, J. F. F., da Rocha Morgado, F. F. and Ferreira, M. E. C., 2017. 'Body image in childhood: An integrative literature review.' *Revista Paulista de Pediatria*, *35*(3), p. 331.

13   Ramseyer Winter, V., Kennedy, A. K. and O'Neill, E., 2017. 'Adolescent tobacco and alcohol use: The influence of body image.' *Journal of Child & Adolescent Substance Abuse*, *26*(3), pp. 219–28.

14   Andreyeva, T., Puhl, R. M. and Brownell, K. D., 2008. 'Changes in perceived weight discrimination among Americans, 1995–1996 through 2004–2006.' *Obesity*, *16*(5), pp. 1129–34; Puhl, R. M., Andreyeva, T. and Brownell, K. D., 2008. 'Perceptions of weight discrimination: Prevalence and comparison to race and gender discrimination in America.' *International Journal of Obesity*, *32*(6), pp. 992–1000; Puhl, R. M. and Heuer, C. A., 2009. 'The stigma of obesity: A review and update. *Obesity*, *17*(5), p. 941.

15   Gov.uk, 17 Oct. 2007. 'Tackling obesities: Future choices. Government Office for Science and Department of Health and Social Care. Retrieved from https://www.gov.uk/government/collections/tackling-obesities-future-choices; Jebb, S., 4 Oct. 2017. 'Dusting off Foresight's obesity report' [blog]. Gov.uk, retrieved from https://foresightprojects.blog.gov.uk/2017/10/04/dusting-off-foresights-obesity-report/.

16   Puhl, R. M. and Latner, J. D., 2007. 'Stigma, obesity, and the health of the nation's children.' *Psychological Bulletin*, *133*(4), p. 557.

17   Richardson, S. A., Goodman, N., Hastorf, A. H. and Dornbusch, S. M., 1961. 'Cultural uniformity in reaction to physical disabilities.' *American Sociological Review*, pp. 241–7.

18   Latner, J. D. and Stunkard, A. J., 2003. 'Getting worse: The stigmatization of obese children.' *Obesity Research*, *11*(3), pp. 452–6.

19   Stice, E., Maxfield, J. and Wells, T., 2003. 'Adverse effects of social pressure to be thin on young women: An experimental investigation of the effects of "fat talk".' *International Journal of Eating Disorders*, *34*(1), pp. 108–17; Durso, L. E., Latner, J. D. and Ciao, A. C., 2016. 'Weight bias internalization in treatment-seeking overweight adults: Psychometric validation and associations with self-esteem, body image, and mood symptoms.' *Eating Behaviors*, *21*, pp. 104–8; O'Brien, K. S., Latner, J. D., Puhl, R. M., Vartanian, L. R., Giles,

C., Griva, K. and Carter, A., 2016. 'The relationship between weight stigma and eating behavior is explained by weight bias internalization and psychological distress.' *Appetite, 102*, pp. 70–6; Pierce, J. W. and Wardle, J., 1997. 'Cause and effect beliefs and self-esteem of overweight children.' *Journal of Child Psychology and Psychiatry, 38*(6), pp. 645–50.

20 Eisenberger, N. I., Lieberman, M. D. and Williams, K. D., 2003. 'Does rejection hurt? An fMRI study of social exclusion.' *Science, 302*(5643), pp. 290–2.

21 Connolly, A. M., Baker, A. and Fellows, C., 13 Jul. 2017. 'Understanding health inequalities in England.' Public Health England. Retrieved from https://publichealthmatters.blog.gov. uk/2017/07/13/understanding-health-inequalities-in-england/.

22 The Marmot Review, Feb. 2010. 'Fair society, healthy lives.' Retrieved from http://www.instituteofhealthequity.org/resources-reports/fair-society-healthy-lives-the-marmot-review/fair-society-healthy-lives-full-report-pdf.pdf.

23 The Health Foundation, Feb. 2020. 'Health equity in England: The Marmot Review 10 years on.' Retrieved from https://www.health. org.uk/publications/reports/the-marmot-review-10-years-on.

24 Bacon, L., 2010. *Health at Every Size*. BenBella Books.

25 Bacon, L. and Aphramor, L., 2011. 'Weight science: Evaluating the evidence for a paradigm shift.' *Nutrition Journal, 10*(1), p. 9.

Chapter 4

1 *New York Times*, 5 Jun. 1967. 'Curves have their day in park; 500 at a "fat-in" call for obesity.' Retrieved from https://www.nytimes.com/ 1967/06/05/archives/curves-have-their-day-in-park-500-at-a-fatin-call-for-obesity.html.

2 Louderback, L., 4 Nov. 1967. 'More people should be FAT.' *Saturday Evening Post*, issue 22.

3 National Association to Advance Fat Acceptance. https://naafa.org/.

4 The Fawcett Society, 7 Mar. 2019. 'Gender stereotypes in early childhood: A literature review.' Retrieved from https://www. fawcettsociety.org.uk/gender-stereotypes-in-early-childhood-a-literature-review.

5 Corner, L. 'Reclaiming the word "queer": What does it mean in 2019?' *Gay Times*. Retrieved from https://gaytimes.co.uk/life/ reclaiming-the-word-queer-what-does-it-mean-in-2019/.

6 Webb, J. B., Rogers, C. B., Etzel, L. and Padro, M. P., 2018. '"Mom, quit fat talking – I'm trying to eat (mindfully) here!": Evaluating a sociocultural model of family fat talk, positive body image, and mindful eating in college women.' *Appetite, 126*, pp. 169–75.

7   Winerman, L., 2006. 'Talking the pain away.' *Monitor on Psychology*, *37*(9), p. 35.

8 Willcox, G., 1982. 'The feeling wheel: A tool for expanding awareness of emotions and increasing spontaneity and intimacy.' *Transactional Analysis Journal*, *12*(4), pp. 274–6.

Chapter 5

1   Tribole, E. and Resch, E., 2020. *Intuitive Eating: A Revolutionary Anti-diet Approach*. Essentials [fourth edition].

2   Orrell-Valente, J. K., Hill, L. G., Brechwald, W. A., Dodge, K. A., Pettit, G. S. and Bates, J. E., 2007. '"Just three more bites": An observational analysis of parents' socialization of children's eating at mealtime.' *Appetite*, *48*(1), pp. 37–45.

3   Satter, E., 2019. 'Division of responsibility in feeding.' The Ellyn Satter Institute. Retrieved from https://www.ellynsatterinstitute. org/how-to-feed/the-division-of-responsibility-in-feeding/.

4   Harbec, M. J. and Pagani, L. S., 2018. 'Associations between early family meal environment quality and later well-being in school-age children. *Journal of Developmental & Behavioral Pediatrics*, *39*(2), pp. 136–43.

5   Harrison, M. E., Norris, M. L., Obeid, N., Fu, M., Weinstangel, H. and Sampson, M., 2015. 'Systematic review of the effects of family meal frequency on psychosocial outcomes in youth.' *Canadian Family Physician*, *61*(2), pp. e96–106.

6   Ibid.

7   DeCosta, P., Møller, P., Frøst, M. B. and Olsen, A., 2017. 'Changing children's eating behaviour – A review of experimental research. *Appetite*, *113*, pp. 327–57.

8   Fernandez, C., McCaffery, H., Miller, A. L., Kaciroti, N., Lumeng, J. C. and Pesch, M. H., 2020. 'Trajectories of picky eating in low-income US children.' *Pediatrics*, *145*(6), p. e20192018.

9   Lumeng, J. C., Miller, A. L., Appugliese, D., Rosenblum, K. and Kaciroti, N., 2018. 'Picky eating, pressuring feeding, and growth in toddlers.' *Appetite*, *123*, pp. 299–305.

10   Maier, A., Chabanet, C., Schaal, B., Issanchou, S. and Leathwood, P., 2007. 'Effects of repeated exposure on acceptance of initially disliked vegetables in 7-month old infants.' *Food Quality and Preference*, *18*(8), pp. 1023–32.

11   Satter, E. M., 2014. 'Testing Satter's Division of Responsibility in Feeding in the context of restrictive snack-management practices.' *The American Journal of Clinical Nutrition*, *100*(3), pp. 986–7.

12   Sugar, R., 22 Oct. 2018. 'Why "natural" food has become a secular stand-in for goodness and purity.' Vox.com. Retrieved

from https://www.vox.com/the-goods/2018/10/22/18009468/
alan-levinovitz-natural-food-morality.

13   DeCosta, P., Møller, P., Frøst, M. B. and Olsen, A., 2017. 'Changing
children's eating behaviour – A review of experimental research.'
Appetite, *113*, pp. 327–57.

14   The Trussell Trust. 'End of year stats.' Retrieved from https://www.
trusselltrust.org/news-and-blog/latest-stats/end-year-stats/.

15   Weal, R., 9 Jul. 2020. '"Eat out to help out" – But what about those
going hungry at home?' The Trussell Trust. Retrieved from https://
www.trusselltrust.org/2020/07/09/eat-out-to-help-out/.

16   University of Oxford, King's College London and The Trussell
Trust Foodbank Network, Jun. 2017. 'Financial insecurity, food
insecurity, and disability: The profile of people receiving emergency
food assistance from The Trussell Trust Foodbank Network in
Britain.' Retrieved from https://www.trusselltrust.org/wp-
content/uploads/sites/2/2017/06/UO_exec_summary_final_02_
04_online.pdf.

17   Corfe, S., 12 Oct. 2018. 'What are the barriers to eating healthily in
the UK?' Social Market Foundation. Retrieved from https://www.
smf.co.uk/publications/barriers-eating-healthily-uk/.

18   United States Department of Agriculture Economic Research
Service, Jun. 2009. 'Access to affordable and nutritious food:
Measuring and understanding food deserts and their consequences.'
Retrieved from https://www.ers.usda.gov/webdocs/publications/
42711/12716_ap036_1_.pdf.

19   Yeh, M. C. and Katz, D. L., 2006. 'Food, nutrition and the health
of urban populations.' *Cities and the Health of the Public*, *1*, p. 106.

20   Brones, A., 7 May 2018. 'Karen Washington: It's not a food desert,
it's food apartheid.' *Guernica*. Retrieved from https://www.
guernicamag.com/karen-washington-its-not-a-food-desert-its-
food-apartheid/.

21   Hastings, G., Stead, M., McDermott, L., Forsyth, A., MacKintosh,
A. M., Rayner, M., Godfrey, C., Caraher, M. and Angus, K., 22 Sep.
2003. 'Review of research on the effects of food promotion to children.'
Centre for Social Marketing, University of Strathclyde. Retrieved
from https://www.researchgate.net/publication/242490173_Review_
Of_Research_On_The_Effects_Of_Food_Promotion_To_Children;
Kraak, V. I. and Story, M., 2015. 'Influence of food companies' brand
mascots and entertainment companies' cartoon media characters on
children's diet and health: A systematic review and research needs.'
Obesity Reviews, *16*(2), pp. 107–26.

22   Birch, L., Savage, J. S. and Ventura, A., 2007. 'Influences on the
development of children's eating behaviours: From infancy to

adolescence.' *Canadian Journal of Dietetic Practice and Research*, *68*(1), pp. s1–56.

23 Robinson, E., Aveyard, P., Daley, A., Jolly, K., Lewis, A., Lycett, D. and Higgs, S., 2013. 'Eating attentively: A systematic review and meta-analysis of the effect of food intake memory and awareness on eating.' *The American Journal of Clinical Nutrition*, *97*(4), pp. 728–42; Francis, L. A. and Birch, L. L., 2008. 'Does eating during television viewing affect preschool children's intake?' *Journal of the American Dietetic Association*, *106*(4), pp. 598–600.

24 Nanney, M. S., Johnson, S., Elliott, M. and Haire-Joshu, D., 2007. 'Frequency of eating homegrown produce is associated with higher intake among parents and their preschool-aged children in rural Missouri.' *Journal of the American Dietetic Association*, *107*(4), pp. 577–84.

Chapter 6

1 Homan, K. J. and Tylka, T. L., 2014. 'Appearance-based exercise motivation moderates the relationship between exercise frequency and positive body image.' *Body Image*, *11*(2), pp. 101–8.

2 Gomes, R., Gonçalves, S. and Costa, J., 2015. 'Exercise, eating disordered behaviors and psychological well-being: A study with Portuguese adolescents.' *Revista Latinoamericana de Psicología*, *47*(1), pp. 66–74.

3 DiBartolo, P. M., Lin, L., Montoya, S., Neal, H. and Shaffer, C., 2007. 'Are there "healthy" and "unhealthy" reasons for exercise? Examining individual differences in exercise motivations using the function of exercise scale.' *Journal of Clinical Sport Psychology*, *1*(2), pp. 93–120.

4 Schoeppe, S., Vandelanotte, C., Bere, E., Lien, N., Verloigne, M., Kovács, É., Manios, Y., Bjelland, M., Vik, F. N. and Van Lippevelde, W., 2017. 'The influence of parental modelling on children's physical activity and screen time: Does it differ by gender?' *The European Journal of Public Health*, *27*(1), pp. 152–7.

5 Rivas, M., 11 Jun. 2019. 'The real issue with Nike's plus size mannequins.' Refinery29. Retrieved from https://www.refinery29.com/en-us/2019/06/235033/nike-plus-size-mannequins-controversy.

6 Wickramasinghe, C. D., Ayers, C. R., Das, S., de Lemos, J. A., Willis, B. L. and Berry, J. D., 2014. 'Prediction of 30-year risk for cardiovascular mortality by fitness and risk factor levels: The Cooper Center Longitudinal Study.' *Circulation: Cardiovascular Quality and Outcomes*, *7*(4), pp. 597–602.

7 Ebbeck, V. and Austin, S., 2018. 'Burning off the fat oppression: Self-compassion exercises for personal trainers.' *Fat Studies*, *7*(1), pp. 81–92.

8   Prichard, I. and Tiggemann, M., 2008. 'Relations among exercise type, self-objectification, and body image in the fitness centre environment: The role of reasons for exercise.' *Psychology of Sport and Exercise*, *9*(6), pp. 855–66.

9   Engeln, R., Shavlik, M. and Daly, C., 2018. 'Tone it down: How fitness instructors' motivational comments shape women's body satisfaction.' *Journal of Clinical Sport Psychology*, *12*(4), pp. 508–24.

10   Faith, M. S., Leone, M. A., Ayers, T. S., Heo, M. and Pietrobelli, A., 2002. 'Weight criticism during physical activity, coping skills, and reported physical activity in children.' *Pediatrics*, *110*(2), p. e23.

11   Be Real, 17 Jan. 2017. 'Somebody like me: A report investigating the impact of body image anxiety in young people in the UK.' Retrieved from https://www.berealcampaign.co.uk/research/somebody-like-me.

12   Nutter, S., Ireland, A., Alberga, A. S., Brun, I., Lefebvre, D., Hayden, K. A. and Russell-Mayhew, S., 2019. 'Weight bias in educational settings: A systematic review.' *Current Obesity Reports*, *8*(2), pp. 185–200.

13   O'Brien, K. S., Hunter, J. A. and Banks, M., 2007. 'Implicit anti-fat bias in physical educators: Physical attributes, ideology and socialization.' *International Journal of Obesity*, *31*(2), pp. 308–14.

14   Greenleaf, C. and Weiller, K., 2005. 'Perceptions of youth obesity among physical educators.' *Social Psychology of Education*, *8*(4), pp. 407–23.

15   Bauer, K. W., Yang, Y. W. and Austin, S. B., 2004. '"How can we stay healthy when you're throwing all of this in front of us?" Findings from focus groups and interviews in middle schools on environmental influences on nutrition and physical activity.' *Health Education & Behavior*, *31*(1), pp. 34–46.

16   Green, L., 2017. *Big Fit Girl*. Greystone Books.

17   Sport England, Dec. 2019. 'Active lives children and young people survey: Academic year 2018/19.' Retrieved from https://sportengland-production-files.s3.eu-west-2.amazonaws.com/s3fs-public/active-lives-children-survey-academic-year-18-19.pdf.

18   UK Active, 2018. 'Generation inactive 2: Nothing about us, without us.' Retrieved from https://www.ukactive.com/wp-content/uploads/2018/09/Generation_Inactive-2_Nothing_About_Us_Without_Us.pdf.

Chapter 7

1   Kemp, S., 21 Jul. 2020. 'Digital 2020: July global statshot.' DataReportal. Retrieved from https://datareportal.com/reports/digital-2020-july-global-statshot.

ENDNOTES

2   American Academy of Child and Adolescent Psychiatry, Mar. 2018. 'Social media and teens.' Retrieved from https://www.aacap.org/ AACAP/Families_and_Youth/Facts_for_Families/FFF-Guide/ Social-Media-and-Teens-100.

3   Eckler, P., Kalyango, Y. and Paasch, E., 2017. 'Facebook use and negative body image among US college women.' *Women & Health*, *57*(2), pp. 249–67; Hogue, J. V. and Mills, J. S., 2019. 'The effects of active social media engagement with peers on body image in young women.' *Body Image*, *28*, pp. 1–5; Dumas, A. A. and Desroches, S., 2019. 'Women's use of social media: What is the evidence about their impact on weight management and body image?' *Current Obesity Reports*, *8*(1), pp. 18–32; Fardouly, J., Diedrichs, P. C., Vartanian, L. R. and Halliwell, E., 2015. 'Social comparisons on social media: The impact of Facebook on young women's body image concerns and mood.' *Body Image*, *13*, pp. 38–45; Salk, R. H. and Engeln-Maddox, R., 2011. '"If you're fat, then I'm humongous!" Frequency, content, and impact of fat talk among college women.' *Psychology of Women Quarterly*, *35*(1), pp. 18–28.

4   Cohen, R., Newton-John, T. and Slater, A., 2020. 'The case for body positivity on social media: Perspectives on current advances and future directions.' *Journal of Health Psychology*, doi: 10.1177/1359105320912450; Cohen, R., Fardouly, J., Newton-John, T. and Slater, A., 2019. '# BoPo on Instagram: An experimental investigation of the effects of viewing body positive content on young women's mood and body image.' *New Media & Society*, *21*(7), pp. 1546–64.

5   Rajanala, S., Maymone, M. B. and Vashi, N. A., 2018. 'Selfies – living in the era of filtered photographs. *JAMA Facial Plastic Surgery*, *20*(6), pp. 443–4.

6   Common Sense Media, 26 Jun. 2012. 'Social media, social life: How teens view their digital lives, 2012.' Retrieved from https://www.commonsensemedia.org/research/ social-media-social-life-how-teens-view-their-digital-lives-2012.

7   Murthy, V. H., 2020. *Together: Loneliness, Health and What Happens When We Find Connection*. Profile Books Ltd.

8   Rose, H., 2019. *You Are Enough*. Aster.

9   Erikson, E. H., 1968. *Identity: Youth and Crisis*. Norton.

10 Sport England. 'This Girl Can campaign summary.' Retrieved from https://sportengland-production-files.s3.eu-west-2. amazonaws.com/s3fs-public/2020-01/Campaign-Summary. pdf?Yu_jmNiqPxjL8IlJC0EqvKXjJ_GOFpfx.

11 Cohen, R., Fardouly, J., Newton-John, T. and Slater, A., 2019. '#BoPo on Instagram: An experimental investigation of the effects

of viewing body positive content on young women's mood and body image.' *New Media & Society, 21*(7), pp. 1546–64.

12   Latzer, Y., Spivak-Lavi, Z. and Katz, R., 2015. 'Disordered eating and media exposure among adolescent girls: The role of parental involvement and sense of empowerment.' *International Journal of Adolescence and Youth, 20*(3), pp. 375–91.

13   Tamir, D. I. and Mitchell, J. P., 2012. 'Disclosing information about the self is intrinsically rewarding.' *Proceedings of the National Academy of Sciences, 109*(21), pp. 8038–43.

Chapter 8

1   Owen, J. and Murphy, M., 20 Jan. 2013. 'Toys Really R Us! How games reflect British culture.' *Independent.* Retrieved from https://www.independent.co.uk/life-style/gadgets-and-tech/news/toys-really-r-us-how-games-reflect-british-culture-8458697.html.

2   Bedford, E., 13 Nov. 2020. 'Toy industry – Statistics & facts.' Statista. Retrieved from https://www.statista.com/topics/1108/toy-industry/.

3   Armitage, M., Dec. 2016. 'Play is a child's work – or is it?' [blog]. Retrieved from https://www.marc-armitage.com/blog-archive/play-is-a-childs-work-or-is-it_111s44.

4   Spears Brown, C., 2014. *Parenting Beyond Pink & Blue: How to Raise Your Kids Free of Gender Stereotypes.* Ten Speed Press.

5   Barbie. 'Our history.' Retrieved from https://barbie.mattel.com/en-us/about/our-history.html.

6   Maine, M., 2000. *Body Wars: Making Peace with Women's Bodies: An Activist's Guide.* Gurze Books.

7   Norton, K. I., Olds, T. S., Olive, S. and Dank, S., 1996. 'Ken and Barbie at life size.' *Sex Roles, 34*(3–4), pp. 287–94.

8   Dittmar, H., Halliwell, E. and Ive, S., 2006. 'Does Barbie make girls want to be thin? The effect of experimental exposure to images of dolls on the body image of 5- to 8-year-old girls.' *Developmental Psychology, 42*(2), p. 283.

9   Barbie Media. 'Fast facts.' Retrieved from http://www.barbiemedia.com/about-barbie/fast-facts.

10   Harriger, J. A., Schaefer, L. M., Thompson, J. K. and Cao, L., 2019. 'You can buy a child a curvy Barbie doll, but you can't make her like it: Young girls' beliefs about Barbie dolls with diverse shapes and sizes.' *Body Image, 30*, pp. 107–13.

11   Sehioho, M., 12 Apr. 2018. 'The impact of male action figures and dolls on boys' body image.' 702 Radio. Retrieved from http://www.702.co.za/articles/299419/the-impact-of-male-action-figures-and-dolls-on-boys-body-image.

12 Fulcher, M. and Hayes, A. R., 2017. 'Building a pink dinosaur: The effects of gendered construction toys on girls' and boys' play.' *Sex Roles*, *79*(5–6), pp. 273–84.

13 Reich, S. M., Black, R. W. and Foliaki, T., 2018. 'Constructing difference: LEGO® set narratives promote stereotypic gender roles and play.' *Sex Roles*, *79*(5–6), pp. 285–98.

14 Tzuriel, D. and Egozi, G., 2010. 'Gender differences in spatial ability of young children: The effects of training and processing strategies'. *Child Development*, *81*(5), pp. 1417–30.

Chapter 9

1 Becker, A. E., 2004. 'Television, disordered eating, and young women in Fiji: Negotiating body image and identity during rapid social change.' *Culture, Medicine and Psychiatry*, *28*(4), pp. 533–59.

2 Mental Health Foundation, 3 Jun. 2019. 'Mental Health Foundation criticises new series of Love Island as it releases new statistics about body image and reality TV.' Retrieved from https://www. mentalhealth.org.uk/news/mental-health-foundation-criticises-new-series-love-island-it-releases-new-statistics-about.

3 BBC Sport, 17 Jan. 2020. 'UK Anti-Doping warns young men not to use steroids in pursuit of "ideal" body.' Retrieved from https://www.bbc.co.uk/sport/51151091.

4 Howard, J. B., Skinner, A. C., Ravanbakht, S. N., Brown, J. D., Perrin, A. J., Steiner, M. J. and Perrin, E. M., 2017. 'Obesogenic behavior and weight-based stigma in popular children's movies, 2012 to 2015.' *Pediatrics*, *140*(6), p. e20172126.

5 Eisenberg, M. E., Carlson–McGuire, A., Gollust, S. E. and Neumark–Sztainer, D., 2015. 'A content analysis of weight stigmatization in popular television programming for adolescents.' *International Journal of Eating Disorders*, *48*(6), pp. 759–66.

6 Ofcom, 4 Feb. 2020. 'Children and parents: Media use and attitudes report 2019.' Retrieved from https://www.ofcom.org.uk/__data/assets/pdf_file/0023/190616/children-media-use-attitudes-2019-report.pdf.

7 Revealing Reality, 29 Jan. 2019. 'Life on the small screen: What children are watching and why: A report for Ofcom.' Ofcom. Retrieved from https://www.ofcom.org.uk/__data/assets/pdf_file/0021/134832/Ofcom-childrens-content-review-Publish.pdf.

8 Wan, G., 25 Oct. 2019. 'Gok Wan on the return of *How to Look Good Naked, Loose Women*.' YouTube. Retrieved from https://www.youtube.com/watch?v=t_yljH-rl_A.

9 Rearick, L., 19 Jul. 2018. '"Steven Universe" is putting a spotlight on body confidence and positivity.' *Teen Vogue*. Retrieved from

https://www.teenvogue.com/story/steven-universe-dove-self-esteem-project-bts.

10   Common Sense Media 'What is media literacy, and why is it important?' Retrieved from https://www.commonsensemedia.org/news-and-media-literacy/what-is-media-literacy-and-why-is-it-important.

11   Diergarten, A. K., Möckel, T., Nieding, G. and Ohler, P., 2017. 'The impact of media literacy on children's learning from films and hypermedia.' *Journal of Applied Developmental Psychology*, *48*, pp. 33–41; Geraee, N., Kaveh, M. H., Shojaeizadeh, D. And Tabatabaee, H. R., 2015. 'Impact of media literacy education on knowledge and behavioral intention of adolescents in dealing with media messages according to Stages of Change.' *Journal of Advances in Medical Education & Professionalism*, *3*(1), p. 9–14.

12   Buckingham, D., Banaji, S., Burn, A., Carr, D., Cranmer, S. and Willett, R., Jan. 2005. 'The media literacy of children and young people: A review of the research literature on behalf of Ofcom.' Centre for the Study of Children Youth and Media, Institute of Education.

13   American Academy of Pediatrics. 'Media education.' Retrieved from https://pediatrics.aappublications.org/content/pediatrics/104/2/341.full.pdf; Common Sense Media 'What is media literacy, and why is it important?' Retrieved from https://www.commonsensemedia.org/news-and-media-literacy/what-is-media-literacy-and-why-is-it-important; National Association for Media Literacy Education. 'Building healthy relationships with media: A parent's guide to media literacy.' Retrieved from https://namle.net/wp-content/uploads/2020/09/parent_guide_final.pdf.

14   Duerager, A. and Livingstone, S., 2012. 'How can parents support children's internet safety?' EU Kids Online. Retrieved from https://www.researchgate.net/publication/313011658_How_can_parents_support_children's_internet_safety.

Chapter 10

1   Adam, H. and Galinsky, A. D., 2012. 'Enclothed cognition'. *Journal of experimental Social Psychology*, *48*(4), pp. 918–25.

2   Barr, S., 26 Dec. 2017. 'Lewis Hamilton under fire for telling nephew "boys don't wear princess dresses".' *Independent*. Retrieved from https://www.independent.co.uk/life-style/health-and-families/lewis-hamilton-christmas-nephew-princess-dresses-formula-one-criticism-gender-a8128661.html.

3   Kross, E., Berman, M. G., Mischel, W., Smith, E. E. and Wager, T. D., 2011. 'Social rejection shares somatosensory representations with

physical pain.' *Proceedings of the National Academy of Sciences, 108*(15), pp. 6270–5.

4   Cubacub, S., 'Radical visibility' in Wong, A. [ed.], 2020. *Disability Visiblity: First-Person Stories from the Twenty-First Century.* Crown Books for Young Readers.

5   Fredrickson, B. L., Roberts, T. A., Noll, S. M., Quinn, D. M. and Twenge, J. M., 1998. 'That swimsuit becomes you: Sex differences in self-objectification, restrained eating, and math performance.' *Journal of Personality and Social Psychology, 75*(1), p. 269; Hebl, M. R., King, E. B. and Lin, J., 2004. 'The swimsuit becomes us all: Ethnicity, gender, and vulnerability to self-objectification.' *Personality and Social Psychology Bulletin, 30*(10), pp. 1322–31; Cox, E., Sabiston, C. M., Karlinsky, A., Manzone, J., Neyedli, H. F. and Welsh, T. N., 2020. 'The impact of athletic clothing style and body awareness on motor performance in women.' *Psychonomic Bulletin & Review, 27*, pp. 1025–35; Tiggemann, M. and Andrew, R., 2012. 'Clothes make a difference: The role of self-objectification.' *Sex Roles, 66*(9–10), pp. 646–54.

6   Bestbier, L. and Williams, T. I., 2017. 'The immediate effects of deep pressure on young people with autism and severe intellectual difficulties: Demonstrating individual differences.' *Occupational Therapy International, 2017 Jan 9*, doi: 10.1155/2017/7534972.

Index

INDEX